180 Days of Social-Emotional Learning
for Second Grade

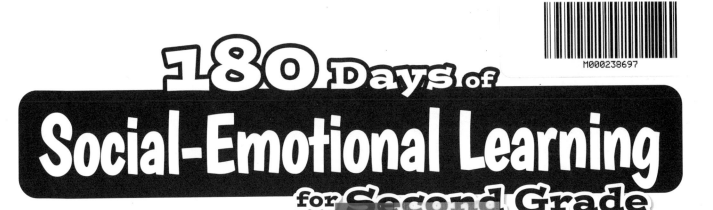

Kris Hinrichsen, M.A.T., NBCT

Consultant

Amy Zoque
Teacher and Instructional Coach
Ontario Montclair School District

Publishing Credits

Corinne Burton, M.A.Ed., *Publisher*
Emily R. Smith, M.A.Ed., *VP of Content Development*
Lynette Ordoñez, *Content Specialist*
David Slayton, *Assistant Editor*
Jill Malcolm, *Multimedia Specialist*

Image Credits: all images from iStock and/or Shutterstock

Social-Emotional Learning Framework

The CASEL SEL framework and competencies were used in the development of this series.
© 2020 The Collaborative for Academic, Social, and Emotional Learning

A division of Teacher Created Materials
5482 Argosy Avenue
Huntington Beach, CA 92649-1039
www.tcmpub.com/shell-education
ISBN 978-1-0876-4971-9
© 2022 Shell Educational Publishing, Inc

Table of Contents

Introduction

"SEL is the process through which all young people and adults acquire and apply the knowledge, skills, and attitudes to develop healthy identities, manage emotions and achieve personal and collective goals, feel and show empathy for others, establish and maintain supportive relationships, and make responsible and caring decisions." (CASEL 2020)

Social-emotional learning (SEL) covers a wide range of skills that help people improve themselves and get fulfilment from their relationships. They are the skills that help propel us into the people we want to be. SEL skills give people the tools to think about the future and manage the day-to-day goal setting to get where we want to be.

The National Commission for Social, Emotional, and Academic Development (2018) noted that children need many skills, attitudes, and values to succeed in school, future careers, and life. "They require skills such as paying attention, setting goals, collaboration and planning for the future. They require attitudes such as internal motivation, perseverance, and a sense of purpose. They require values such as responsibility, honesty, and integrity. They require the abilities to think critically, consider different views, and problem solve." Explicit SEL instruction will help students develop and hone these important skills, attitudes, and values.

Daniel Goleman (2005), a social scientist who popularized SEL, adds, "Most of us have assumed that the kind of academic learning that goes on in school has little or nothing to do with one's emotions or social environment. Now, neuroscience is telling us exactly the opposite. The emotional centers of the brain are intricately interwoven with the neocortical areas involved in cognitive learning." As adults, we may find it difficult to focus on work after a bad day or a traumatic event. Similarly, student learning is impacted by their emotions. By teaching students how to deal with their emotions in a healthy way, they will reap the benefits academically as well.

SEL is doing the work to make sure students can be successful at home, with their friends, at school, in sports, in relationships, and in life. The skills are typically separated into five competencies: self-awareness, self-management, social awareness, relationship skills, and responsible decision-making.

Introduction *(cont.)*

Social-Emotional Competencies

SELF-MANAGEMENT
Manage your emotions, thoughts, and behaviors. Set and work toward goals.

SOCIAL AWARENESS
Take on the perspectives of others, especially those who are different from you. Understand societal expectations and know where to get support.

SELF-AWARENESS
Recognize your own emotions, thoughts, and values. Assess your strengths and weaknesses. Have a growth mindset.

S E L   C O M P E T E N C I E S

RESPONSIBLE DECISION-MAKING
Make positive choices based on established norms. Understand and consider consequences.

RELATIONSHIP SKILLS
Establish and maintain relationships with others. Communicate effectively and negotiate conflict as necessary.

Each SEL competency helps support child development in life-long learning. SEL helps students develop the skills to have rich connections with their emotional lives and build robust emotional vocabularies. These competencies lead to some impressive data to support students being successful in school and in life.

- Students who learn SEL skills score an average of 11 percentage points higher on standardized tests.

- They are less likely to get office referrals and will spend more time in class.

- These students are more likely to want to come to school and report being happier while at school.

- Educators who teach SEL skills report a 77 percent increase in job satisfaction. (Durlack, et al. 2011)

Your SEL Skills

Educators, parents, and caretakers have a huge part to play as students develop SEL skills. Parker Palmer (2007) reminds us that what children do is often a reflection of what they see and experience. When you stay calm, name your feelings, practice clear communication, and problem-solve in a way that students see, then they reflect that modeling in their own relationships. As you guide students in how to handle conflicts, you can keep a growth mindset and know that with practice, your students can master any skill.

Introduction *(cont.)*

Scenarios

There are many benefits to teaching SEL, from how students behave at home to how they will succeed in life. Let's think about how children with strong SEL skills would react to common life experiences.

At Home

Kyle wakes up. He uses self-talk and says to himself, *I am going to do my best today.* He gets out of bed, picks out his own clothes to wear, and gets ready. As he sits down for breakfast, his little sister knocks over his glass of milk. He thinks, *Uggh, she is so messy! But that's ok—it was just an accident.* Then, he tells his parent and helps clean up the mess.

When his parent picks Kyle up from school, Kyle asks how they are feeling and answers questions about how his day has gone. He says that he found the reading lesson hard, but he used deep breathing and asked questions to figure out new words today.

As his family is getting dinner ready, he sees that his parent is making something he really doesn't like. He stomps his foot in protest, and then he goes to sit in his room for a while. When he comes out, he asks if they can make something tomorrow that he likes.

When he is getting ready for bed, he is silly and playful. He wants to read and point out how each person in the book is feeling. His parent asks him how he would handle the problem the character is facing, and then they talk about the situation.

At School

Cynthia gets to school a little late, and she has to check into the office. Cynthia is embarrassed about being late but feels safe at school and knows that the people there will welcome her with kindness. She steps into her room, and her class pauses to welcome her. Her teacher says, "I'm so glad you are here today."

Cynthia settles into her morning work. After a few minutes, she comes to a problem she doesn't know how to solve. After she gives it her best try, she asks her teacher for some help. Her teacher supports her learning, and Cynthia feels proud of herself for trying.

As lunchtime nears, Cynthia realizes she forgot her lunch in the car. She asks her teacher to call her mom. Her mom says she can't get away and that Cynthia is going to have to eat the school lunch today. Cynthia is frustrated but decides that she is not going to let it ruin her day.

As she is getting ready for school to end, her teacher invites the class to reflect about their day. What is something they are proud of? What is something they wished they could do again? Cynthia thinks about her answers and shares with the class.

These are both pretty dreamy children. The reality is that the development of SEL skills happens in different ways. Some days, students will shock you by how they handle a problem. Other times, they will dig in and not use the skills you teach them. One of the benefits of teaching SEL is that when a student is melting down, your mindset shifts to *I wonder how I can help them learn how to deal with this* rather than *I'm going to punish them so they don't do this again.* Viewing discipline as an opportunity to teach rather than punish is critical for students to learn SEL.

How to Use This Book

Using the Practice Pages

This series is designed to support the instruction of SEL. It is not a curriculum. The activities will help students practice, learn, and grow their SEL skills. Each week is set up for students to practice all five SEL competencies.

 Day 1—Self-Awareness

 Day 2—Self-Management

 Day 3—Social Awareness

 Day 4—Relationship Skills

 Day 5—Responsible Decision-Making

Each of the five competencies has subcategories that are used to target specific skills each day. See the chart on pages 10–11 for a list of which skills are used throughout the book.

Each week also has a theme. These themes rotate and are repeated several times throughout the book. The following themes are included in this book:

- self
- friends
- family
- neighborhood
- community
- school

This book also features one week that focuses on online safety.

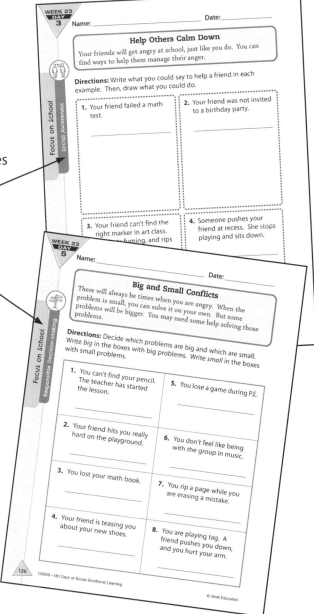

How to Use This Book *(cont.)*

Using the Resources

Rubrics for connecting to self, relating to others, and making decisions can be found on pages 199–201 and in the Digital Resources. Use the rubrics to consider student work. Be sure to share these rubrics with students so that they know what is expected of them.

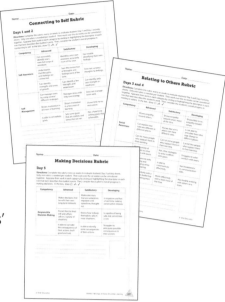

Diagnostic Assessment

Educators can use the pages in this book as diagnostic assessments. The data analysis tools included with this book enable teachers or parents/caregivers to quickly assess students' work and monitor their progress. Educators can quickly see which skills students may need to target further to develop proficiency.

Students will learn how to connect with their own emotions, how to connect with the emotions of others, and how to make good decisions. Assess student learning in each area using the rubrics on pages 199–201. Then, record their overall progress on the analysis sheets on pages 202–204. These charts are also provided in the Digital Resources as PDFs and Microsoft Excel® files.

To Complete the Analyses:

- Write or type students' names in the far-left column. Depending on the number of students, more than one copy of each form may be needed.

- The weeks in which students should be assessed are indicated in the first rows of the charts. Students should be assessed at the ends of those weeks.

- Review students' work for the day(s) indicated in the corresponding rubric. For example, if using the Making Decisions Analysis sheet for the first time, review students' work from Day 5 for all six weeks.

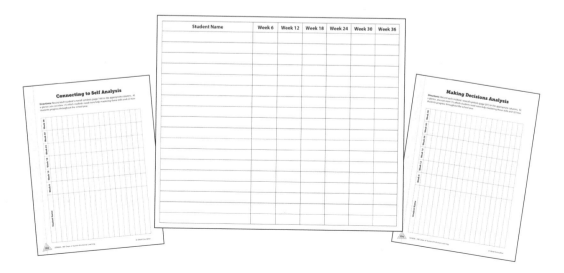

Integrating SEL into Your Teaching

Student self-assessment is key for SEL skills. If students can make accurate evaluations of how they are feeling, then they can work to manage their emotions. If they can manage their emotions, they are more likely to have better relationship skills and make responsible decisions. Children can self-assess from a very young age. The earlier you get them into this practice, the more they will use it and benefit from it for the rest of their lives. The following are some ways you can quickly and easily integrate student self-assessment into your daily routines.

Feelings Check-Ins

Using a scale can be helpful for a quick check-in. After an activity, ask students to rate how they are feeling. Focusing students' attention on how they are feeling helps support their self-awareness. Discuss how students' feelings change as they do different things. Provide students with a visual scale to support these check-ins. These could be taped to their desks or posted in your classroom. Full-color versions of the following scales can be found in the Digital Resources.

- **Emoji:** Having students point to different emoji faces is an easy way to use a rating scale with young students.

- **Symbols:** Symbols, such as weather icons, can also represent students' emotions.

- **Color Wheel:** A color wheel, where different colors represent different emotions, is another effective scale.

- **Numbers:** Have students show 1–5 fingers, with 5 being *I'm feeling great* to 1 being *I'm feeling awful*.

Integrating SEL into Your Teaching *(cont.)*

Reflection

Reflecting is the process of looking closely or deeply at something. When you prompt students with reflection questions, you are supporting this work. Here is a list of questions to get the reflection process started:

- What did you learn from this work?
- What are you proud of in this piece?
- What would you have done differently?
- What was the most challenging part?
- How could you improve this work?
- How did other people help you finish this work?
- How will doing your best on this assignment help you in the future?

Pan Balance

Have students hold out their arms on both sides of their bodies. Ask them a reflection question that has two possible answers. Students should respond by tipping one arm lower than the other (as if one side of the scale is heavier). Here are some example questions:

- Did you talk too much or too little?
- Were you distracted or engaged?
- Did you rush or take too much time?
- Did you stay calm or get angry?
- Was your response safe or unsafe?

Calibrating Student Assessments

Supporting student self-assessment means calibrating their thinking. You will have students who make mistakes but evaluate themselves as though they have never made a mistake in their lives. At the other end of the spectrum, you will likely see students who will be too hard on themselves. In both these cases, having a periodic calibration can help to support accuracy in their evaluations. The *Calibrating Student Assessments* chart is provided in the Digital Resources (calibrating.pdf).

Teaching Assessment

In addition to assessing students, consider the effectiveness of your own instruction. The *Teaching Rubric* can be found in the Digital Resources (teachingrubric.pdf). Use this tool to evaluate your SEL instruction. You may wish to complete this rubric at different points throughout the year to track your progress.

Skills Alignment

Each activity in this book is aligned to a CASEL competency. Within each competency, students will learn a variety of skills. Here are some of the important skills students will practice during the year.

 Self-Awareness

Identifying Emotions	Understanding Problems
Examining Stereotypes and Biases	Connecting Feelings to Actions
Identity	Positivity
Growth Mindset	Feelings Words
Honesty	Using Mantras
Reflection	Examining Impact
Mindfulness	

Self-Management

Managing Emotions	Problem-Solving
Staying Organized	Self-Improvement
Stress Management	Self-Control
Setting Goals	Triggers
Agency	Dealing with Worry
Trying New Things	Bravery
Calming Down	Accepting Losses

 Social Awareness

Thinking about Others	Understanding Others' Feelings
Taking Others' Perspectives	Kindness
Empathy	Helping Others
Gratitude	Working Together
Finding Strengths in Others	Point of View
Fairness	

Skills Alignment *(cont.)*

Relationship Skills	
Making Friends	Leadership
Communication	Solving Conflicts
Standing Up for Oneself and Others	Asking Questions
Teamwork	Supporting Others
Asking for Help	Listening
Helping Others	
Responsible Decision-Making	
Identifying Solutions	Forgiveness
Being Open-Minded	Making Good Choices
Reflection	Solving Problems and Conflicts
Considering Next Steps	Critical Thinking
Thoughtfulness	Celebrating Successes
Apologizing	

Name: _____ Date: _____

Name Your Emotions

It is important to check in with your body. Think about how you feel so you can learn more and do your best.

Directions: Read each event. Think about how you feel while doing the event. Draw a picture to show your face.

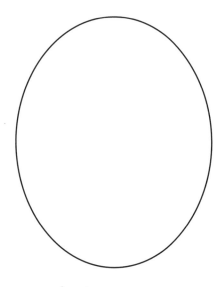

playing a game

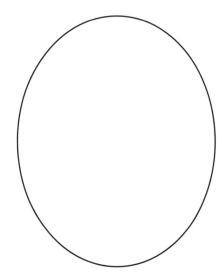

first day of school

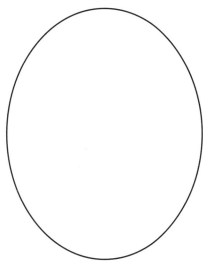

riding a roller coaster

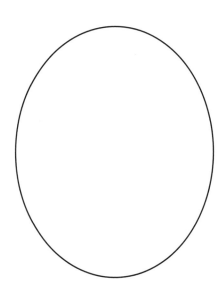

holding a spider

Name: _____ **Date:** _____

Manage Your Emotions

Your emotions can change a lot in one day. There are big emotions, such as getting mad or sad. Those can make it hard to learn. You can help yourself calm down from big emotions. Count backward from 10 to 0 very slowly.

Directions: Point to each number. Say it out loud as you point. Then, color each number and count backward slowly.

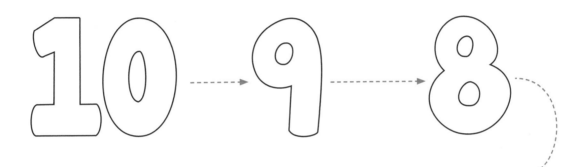

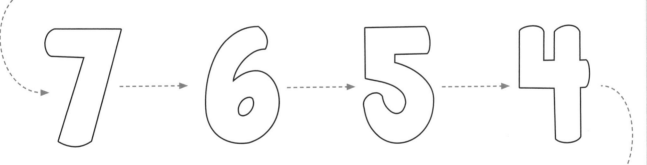

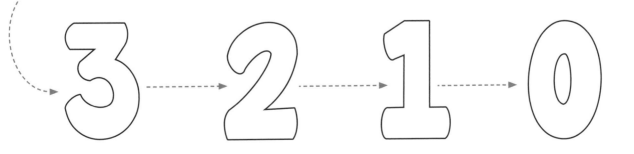

Name: _____ Date: _____

Focus on Self

Social Awareness

Think about Others

Pay attention to how your friends feel. This will make you a better friend.

Directions: Read each story. Write how you think the character is feeling.

Jessica is playing on the swings at recess. She is with her best friend. As she is swinging, Jessica slips off and falls to the ground. Her eyes fill with tears, and she starts to cry.

1. How is Jessica feeling?

_____

_____

Mark is going to a park with his family. They make plans to meet a friend there. When Mark gets to the park, the sun is shining and it's warm. Mark plays with his friend and smiles a lot.

2. How is Mark feeling?

_____

_____

Make Good Friends

Making new friends is exciting. It is one of the best parts of each new school year.

Directions: Color the things that might help you make a new friend.

Ask what someone likes to do for fun.

Tell someone they can't play with you.

Take someone's pencil that they left on the table.

Sit next to someone new at lunch.

Invite someone to play with you at recess.

Tell someone you like their shirt.

Name: _____ Date: _____

Focus on Self

Responsible Decision-Making

Find Solutions

Part of second grade is learning how to solve problems.

Directions: Read the problem. Write about how you think the friends should solve it.

Rosy and Brad both want to play with the basketball at recess. Brad got to the court first, but Rosy got the ball first. What should they do?

1. How should Rosy and Brad solve this problem?

_____

_____

2. Draw a picture to show what they should do.

Name Your Emotions

The people you live with can make you have strong feelings.

Directions: Think about each situation. Write one word to describe how each one would make you feel.

1. Someone in your family takes your snack.

   _____

2. Someone in your family cooks you dinner.

   _____

3. Someone in your family asks if you need help.

   _____

4. Someone in your family takes you to a movie.

   _____

5. Someone in your family rips your shirt.

   _____

6. Someone in your family repeats every word you say.

   _____

7. Someone in your family tells you they love you.

   _____

Focus on Family

Self-Awareness

Name: _____ Date: _____

Manage Your Emotions

It can be hard to calm down when you're upset. There are things you can do to help you relax and feel better.

Directions: Read each statement. Think about how you would feel if each thing happened to you. Match each statement on the left with a response on the right that would help you calm down.

You find your favorite toy in your brother's room.	Take a deep breath, and count back from 10.
Your parent tells you that your friend can't come over.	Talk to your parent about how you feel.
Your parent says you can't watch TV.	Think positive thoughts to yourself.
Your sister won't let you join a game.	Make a tight fist. Imagine the mad leaving your body.

Think about Others

Pay close attention. You may notice when your family needs help to cheer up.

Directions: Study these pictures. Write how you could cheer up each family member.

Focus on Family

Social Awareness

Name: _____ Date: _____

Make Good Choices

Spend time with members of your family. This is a great way to build strong relationships!

Focus on Family

Relationship skills

Directions: Read this list of things you could do with other people at home. Add one of your own at the end. Write an *X* next to three activities you want to try.

☐ Build a blanket fort.   ☐ Paint a picture.

☐ Cook a meal.   ☐ Play a game.

☐ Create something.   ☐ Read a book.

☐ Go for a walk.   ☐ _____

☐ Learn about something.   _____

Directions: Draw a picture that shows you doing one of the activities you want to try.

Find Solutions

Knowing how to stay safe at home is important.

Directions: Each picture shows something unsafe. Each one also shows someone helping. Read about each picture. Then, color each person who is helping.

There is smoke in the house. The family calls 9-1-1. Firefighters come to help.

Someone falls down the steps and breaks their arm. Doctors help.

A car breaks down on the highway. The family calls 9-1-1. The police come to help.

There is an earthquake! The girl gets under a table to stay safe.

Focus on Family

Responsible Decision-Making

Name: _____ Date: _____

Know Yourself

Being a good friend starts with how you see yourself. You can be a better friend if you learn more about who you are.

Directions: Answer each question about you.

1. What is your favorite thing to do?

   _____

   _____

2. What are you good at?

   _____

   _____

3. What do you like to learn about?

   _____

   _____

4. What makes you special?

   _____

   _____

Name: _____ **Date:** _____

Manage Your Emotions

A friend may hurt your feelings. That will cause big emotions. You can deal with those big emotions with self-talk. Self-talk is words or phrases you tell yourself to help calm down.

Here are some examples of self-talk:

- I can do this!
- My friends like me.
- I will do my best!
- I can try again.

Directions: Read each sentence. What self-talk would you use to help you calm down? Write one of the examples, or write your own.

1. You hear someone say something mean about you. You start to get angry.

   _____

   _____

2. Yesterday, someone made fun of your clothes. Today, that person is your partner for a project.

   _____

   _____

3. Your friends don't want to play the game that you want to play.

   _____

   _____

Focus on Friends

Self-Management

Name: _____ Date: _____

Think about Others

When you pay attention to your friends, you will learn what they like. You will also learn what they don't like.

Directions: Read each story. Write what you learn about the people.

Ryan and Donnie are on a bike ride together. They ride by a baseball field. Ryan slams on his brakes. He hops off his bike and jumps up and down. Ryan asks Donnie to watch the game with him.

1. How do you think Ryan feels about baseball?

_____

2. How does he show that?

_____

_____

Hanna is working on an art project. She puts her hands on her head and takes a deep breath. She puts her head down and pushes her paper away.

3. How do you think Hanna feels about this art project?

_____

4. How does she show that?

_____

_____

Focus on Friends Social Awareness

Name: _____ Date: _____

Make Good Friendships

It feels good to help others. Helping also makes friendships stronger.

Directions: Read each example. Draw a picture to show how you could help.

1. You see some trash on the ground.	**3.** A person drops a book.
2. Someone is playing alone.	**4.** Your friend doesn't have a partner for a game.

Name: _____ Date: _____

Find Solutions

A *conflict* is a problem between people. Sometimes, friends have conflicts. When they do, you can help.

Directions: Fill in the letter for the best way to solve each problem.

1.

(A) Throw the dice down, and quit the game.

(B) Play Rock, Paper, Scissors to see who will go first.

3.

(A) Play with the toy together.

(B) Take the toy and run away.

2.

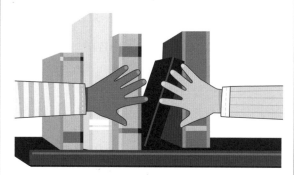

(A) Ask if there is another copy of the book.

(B) Put the book away so no one can read it.

4.

(A) Hide it in the corner.

(B) Tell an adult, and try to make it better.

Name: _____ Date: _____

Benefits of Your Culture

Your culture is made up of everything around you. Culture includes where you live. It also includes what you eat. It includes how you treat your parents and how you spend your time.

Directions: Draw a picture of your family doing each activity.

1. celebrating a birthday

3. making a decision

2. eating dinner

4. going for a walk in your neighborhood

Directions: Now, ask another person how they do each of these. Draw a picture of one that is different from yours.

Name: _____ Date: _____

Stay Organized

Part of being in a community is helping. That can mean a lot of work. Use a checklist to stay organized.

Directions: Circle two things you can do to help. Then, add them to the checklist.

shovel my neighbor's sidewalk

pick up trash at the park

use the sidewalk when I'm walking

take care of a neighbor's pet

volunteer at a homeless shelter

rake my neighbor's leaves

be nice to the kids in my neighborhood

Focus on Community

Self-Management

My Checklist

1. ☐ _____

_____

2. ☐ _____

_____

Take Others' Perspectives

There are many types of communities. Some are like yours. Some are different. It is helpful to notice what is the same and what is different.

Focus on Community

Social Awareness

Directions: Think about where you live. Study each picture. Write one thing that is the same as your community. Write one thing that is different.

Same: _____

_____

Different: _____

_____

Same: _____

_____

Different: _____

_____

Same: _____

_____

Different: _____

_____

Name: _____ **Date:** _____

Stand Up for the Rights of Others

People are treated unfairly sometimes. It is important to stand up for them.

Directions: Circle the pictures of things that are fair. Write an *X* through each one that is not fair.

Directions: Choose one of the pictures that is not fair. Draw a way to make it fair.

Name: _____ **Date:** _____

Identify Solutions

You can prevent many problems by making good choices. But problems can still happen.

Directions: There is a problem in each picture. Circle the bad decision. Then, write a solution.

_____

_____

_____

_____

_____

_____

Focus on Community

Responsible Decision-Making

Name: _____ Date: _____

Identifying Emotions

Your body will let you know when you have big feelings.

Focus on Self

Self-Awareness

Directions: Each picture shows a big feeling. Write one thing each body is doing to show the feeling.

mad

1. _____

   _____

happy

2. _____

   _____

sad

3. _____

   _____

scared

4. _____

   _____

Deal with Stress

Stress can cause our bodies to act in different ways. Most of them don't feel very good. Finding ways to lower our stress can help us feel better.

Directions: This is one activity to release stress. Work through each step. Then, think about how your body feels.

Drain the Bucket

Step 1

Pretend you are holding a bucket with both hands. Pretend it is filled with feathers. Squeeze your hands like they are around the handle. Pick up the bucket. Count down from five. Put the bucket back down. Relax your hands.

Step 2

Pretend you are holding a bucket with both hands. Pretend it is filled with rocks. Squeeze your hands like they are around the handle. Pick up the bucket. Count down from five. Put the bucket back down. Relax your hands.

Step 3

Check in. Circle how your body feels.

Self-Management

Focus on Self

Name: _____ Date: _____

Focus on Self

Social Awareness

Show Empathy

Being kind and helpful to others can make us feel proud.

Directions: Read each description. How could you help in each situation? Draw a picture to show how. Then, answer the question.

1. You see someone playing alone at the park.

3. You see a friend crying.

2. Someone falls down in the hall.

4. Someone spills their lunch on the floor.

5. How can you be kind and helpful today?

_____

_____

Name: _____ Date: _____

Communicate Well

Communication is when people tell each other things. You don't have to use words though. Your actions can tell people things. Your body can tell people things, too. This is called *nonverbal communication*.

Directions: Look at the picture of the sad child. Write what you see each body part doing.

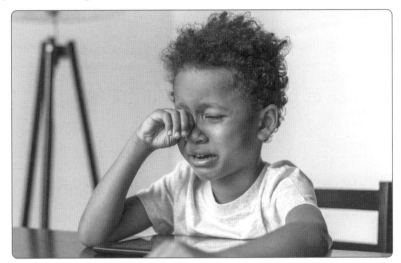

eyes: _____

mouth: _____

hand: _____

Directions: Think about what your body does when you are sad. Then, finish each sentence.

My eyes _____.

My mouth _____.

My hands _____.

Name: _____ Date: _____

Be Open-Minded

Being open to new things means that you are willing to try new things. Trying new things can lead you to find new things you like to do.

Directions: Read each type of activity. Write something new you would like to try. Choose one from the list, or write your own.

1. sports, such as karate, soccer, yoga, or ballet

   _____

2. activities, such as building, fixing, or traveling

   _____

3. games, such as chess, checkers, or a card game

   _____

Directions: Draw a picture of yourself doing one of the new things.

Name: _____ **Date:** _____

Be Fair

Sometimes, people treat others differently because of how they look or act. It is not fair. We should treat people fairly.

Directions: Find the things that are unfair. Write an *X* through each.

You see a boy from your class sitting at a table alone. You invite him to eat with you.

A boy tells a girl that she can't play football with them. Only boys play football.

A girl takes a doll away from a boy. Only girls play with dolls.

A kid from the apartment across the street asks to play. You say yes.

Challenge: Notice how the people you see are being treated. Is it fair? At the end of the day, tell someone what you saw. Think of one thing that was unfair.

Name: _____ Date: _____

Set Up Goals

Setting a goal is when you think about something you want to do. Then, you make a plan to do it.

Directions: The kids in your neighborhood want to set up a clubhouse. First, you need to make a plan. Write each step of the plan. Then, draw the clubhouse on another sheet of paper.

Step 1

Where is the clubhouse going to be?

_____

Step 2

What supplies do you need?

_____

_____

Step 3

Who is going to help you?

_____

_____

Step 4

How will you know when it's finished?

_____

_____

Focus on Neighborhood

Self-Management

Name: _____ Date: _____

Be Thankful

Saying thank you when others do nice things for us is a great way to build a strong neighborhood. It helps you feel good, too.

Directions: Read each way to say thank you. Color the ones you would like to try this week.

Write a letter.

Draw a picture of someone.

Make something special.

Bake cookies.

Say thank you.

Write a poem or song.

Offer to help with a project.

Bring flowers.

Directions: Answer the questions.

1. Who can you say thank you to this week?

   _____

2. How did that person help you?

   _____

   _____

3. How will you say thank you?

   _____

   _____

Name: _____ Date: _____

Focus on Neighborhood

Relationship Skills

Understand Your Culture

People in a group can have a lot in common. This is called *culture*. Food is one part of culture. Language is another. Clothes and music are also part of culture. So are holidays.

Directions: Write your favorite meal. Meet with a partner. Answer the questions.

1. My favorite meal is _____.

2. My partner's favorite meal is _____.

3. How are your foods the same? How are they different?

_____

_____

_____

Directions: Draw a picture of you and your partner sharing a meal.

Name: _____ Date: _____

Think about Your Choices

It can be hard to make good choices. Thinking about what might happen can help you decide what to do.

Directions: Write what might happen in each example.

1. What might happen if a car comes by?

_____

_____

_____

2. What might happen if this kid falls off the bike?

_____

_____

_____

3. What might happen if water spills on the computer?

_____

_____

_____

Name: _____ Date: _____

Your Identity

Your identity is how you see yourself. You can have one identity at home and one at school. Seeing yourself as a good person can be part of it.

Directions: Read the words in the Word Bank. Then, use the words to complete the Venn diagram. Add words of your own, too.

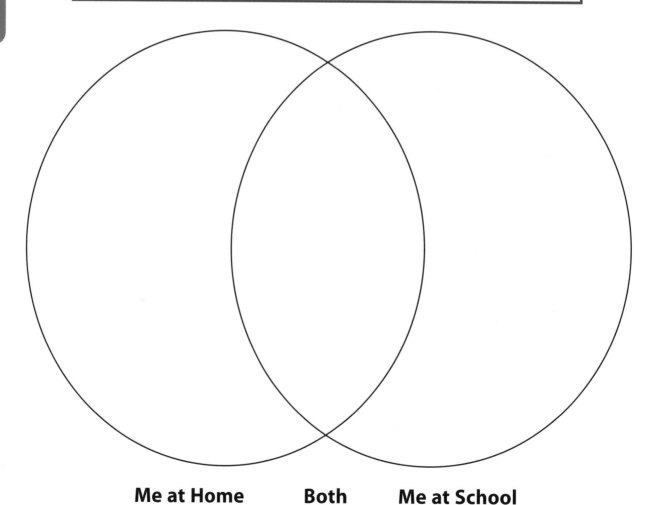

Word Bank

| careful | fair | helpful | loving |
| caring | friendly | kind | respectful |

Me at Home   **Both**   **Me at School**

Name: _____ **Date:** _____

Set Goals

Your identity is how you see yourself. But your actions show people who you are. Setting goals can help show people you are kind.

Directions: You want to be kind. Choose three things from this list that you would like to do. Or choose your own. Then, answer the questions.

Things to Do for Others

Invite someone to play with you.   Offer to help someone.

Help clean something up.   Make something for a friend.

Say something nice to someone.   Hold a door open for someone.

1. Which three things will you do?

_____

_____

_____

2. Who will you do each thing for?

_____

_____

_____

Name: _____ **Date:** _____

Find Strengths in Others

Take time to learn what your friends do well. This can help you be a better friend.

Focus on School

Social Awareness

Directions: Think of two friends. Answer the questions about each one.

What is your friend's name? _____

What are they really good at? _____

_____

_____

What do they like to do? _____

_____

What is your friend's name? _____

What are they really good at? _____

_____

_____

What do they like to do? _____

_____

Name: _____ Date: _____

Communication

Communication happens all the time. It happens a lot at school. Your teachers do it when they teach. You do it when you talk with friends. Listening is a big part of communication. Being a good listener takes a lot of work. You can get better at it with practice.

Focus on School

Relationship Skills

Directions: Color each picture after you read how to be a better listener.

1. Keep your eyes on the speaker.

2. Keep your ears listening.

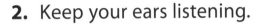

3. Keep your mouth closed.

4. Keep your body calm.

5. Keep your mind tuned in.

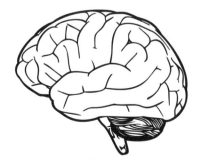

Name: _____ Date: _____

Solve Problems

Big and small problems happen at school. Big problems need an adult to help solve them. Small problems are ones that you can solve.

Directions: Decide whether each problem is big or small. Draw an arrow from each problem to the big side or the small side.

Big Problems	Problems	Small Problems
	Kelly takes your pencil.	
	You see smoke coming from a tablet.	
	Mayra falls and breaks her foot.	
	Aimee is thirsty.	
	Javier takes food from your lunch.	
	Perry can't find his boot.	

Directions: Bekkah and Dante are at recess. They both get to the slide at the same time. They each want to be the first one down the slide. How can they solve this problem?

_____

_____

_____

Name: _____ Date: _____

Find Things You Like

Your community has a lot of things to do. Trying new things can be hard. But you might find something you love to do.

Directions: Circle the things you know you like. Draw squares around the things you would like to try.

flag football

ballet

music lessons

going to a mall

baseball

soccer

gymnastics

fishing

tae kwon do

karate

Directions: Draw a picture of you doing a new thing.

Name: _____   Date: _____

Agency

To stand up for yourself or others is called *agency*. It takes a lot of courage to do this. It also takes practice.

Directions: Read the story. Then, answer the questions.

Layla lives in a small community. She loves walking to school every day. She starts to see trash on the sidewalk. She asks her dad if there is anything she can do to help. Her dad says, "Yes, our family can go pick up trash. We will wear gloves and take a trash bag to pick up all the trash we see."

1. What problem did Layla see?

_____

_____

2. Who did she tell?

_____

3. How did they solve the problem?

_____

_____

Name: _____ Date: _____

Rules in Different Places

Different places have their own rules. Knowing what those rules are will help you have more fun.

Directions: Write how you can stay safe in each place.

Swimming Pool	**School**
_____	_____
_____	_____
_____	_____
Public Library	**Home**
_____	_____
_____	_____
_____	_____

Focus on Community

Social Awareness

Name: _____ Date: _____

Stand Up for Yourself

Sometimes, friends will do things that you know are wrong. They might even ask you to join them. This is called *peer pressure*. It can be hard to do what is right when your friends pressure you to do something wrong.

Directions: Write what you would say to each person.

1. You and Jesse see a skateboard next to a bench. He tells you to take it.

   _____

   _____

2. Shawn offers you a piece of gum he stole from a store.

   _____

   _____

3. Kaylee asks you to take money from your parent's wallet.

   _____

   _____

4. Miles makes fun of Alex and asks you to join in.

   _____

   _____

Name: _____ Date: _____

Strong Communities

A strong community can make life better.

Directions: Write how each of these places can make your life better.

How do parks make life better?

_____

_____

How do libraries make life better?

_____

_____

How do basketball courts make life better?

_____

_____

How do pools and waterparks make life better?

_____

_____

Name: _____ **Date:** _____

Focus on Self

Self-Awareness

Growth Mindset

A growth mindset is the idea that an open mind can help you learn new things. People who try hard have a growth mindset. They think they can do new things. People who don't try sometimes have a fixed mindset. They think they can't do new things. Keeping a growth mindset with good self-talk can help you reach your goals.

Directions: Read the phrases in the box. Some are positive things you should say for self-talk. Some are things you should not say. Sort them into the table.

Use for Self-Talk	Don't Use for Self-Talk

I am going to fail.	I can learn how to do this.
I am going to keep trying.	I can't do this.
I am not that smart.	I will try a different way.
I believe in myself.	Learning is fun.
I can do hard things.	This is too hard.

Set Goals

Goals can be big or small. What you want to be when you grow up is a big goal. Something you can do today is a small goal. It's good to have both types of goals. This will help you stay motivated and get things done.

Directions: Choose one of these small goals, or write your own. Circle one you can work on today.

Set a Small Goal

Read for 30 minutes.

Count by 2s to 100.

Write for 15 minutes.

Do my chores without being asked.

Make 10 basketball shots.

_____

_____

Directions: Write your goal. Give yourself an *X* every day you meet it. Try to get five *X*s this week. Then, make your own chart for next week. Put the charts somewhere you will see them.

My Goal: _____

_____

Mon.	Tues.	Wed.	Thurs.	Fri.

Self-Management

Focus on Self

Name: _____   Date: _____

Ask for Help

When you work to get better at something, it helps to ask for help. Knowing who to ask for help is an important skill.

Directions: Read each problem. Draw a line to the best helper. Helpers can be used more than once.

Problems

Helpers

You can't find a book to read.

parent or caretaker

You need help finding a clean pair of socks.

teacher

You are looking for someone to play with.

librarian

You broke a window at your house.

sibling or cousin

You ran out of paper at school.

best friend

Name: _____ Date: _____

Teamwork

It can be hard to do new things alone. Working as a team can make it easier to get better.

Directions: Read the story. Then, list three things James does better because of his team.

James wants to get better at soccer, so he joins a team. His coach teaches him how to kick the ball on the inside of his foot. This gives him more control. His teammate runs with him, and James runs faster to catch up. When James scores a goal, his friend gives him a high-five. James feels proud.

1. _____

2. _____

3. _____

Name: _____   Date: _____

Focus on Self

Responsible Decision-Making

Reflection

A big step to reach your goals is to reflect. To reflect is to think about how you are doing and how you are feeling.

Directions: Think about a skill you worked on this week. It could be reading or math. It could be a hobby or a sport. Then, answer the questions to reflect.

1. What did you do?

_____

2. What did you learn?

_____

_____

3. What did you do well?

_____

_____

4. What could you have done better?

_____

_____

5. How do you feel about your work? Circle one.

Name: _____ Date: _____

Be Honest

We all make mistakes. It can be hard to tell the truth when that happens. But it always feels better to be honest. It also makes our relationships stronger.

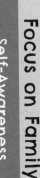

Focus on Family

Self-Awareness

Directions: Read each story. Then, draw what you think each person should do.

1. Zoey is playing with her sister's doll. As she moves the arm, it breaks off. She tries to fix it, but it won't go back on.

2. Alice is playing ball outside. She kicks the ball harder than she wanted to. It hits a window and cracks it.

Name: _____ Date: _____

Show Courage to Help

Finding ways to help your family can be a lot of work. It takes courage to help before being asked.

Directions: Study each picture. Write what you could do to help.

1. _____

_____

2. _____

_____

3. _____

_____

Directions: Draw one new thing you could do to help your family without being asked.

Name: _____ Date: _____

Ways to Say Thank You

It's good to thank people when they do nice things. It makes them feel good about what they did. There are many ways to say thank you. One way is to write a note.

Directions: Read the nice things that people did. Write a thank you note for each one.

Example

Kent's mom made his favorite breakfast.

Mom, thank you for making me pancakes.

1. Hazel's brother helped her clean up a big mess.

   _____

   _____

2. Jordan's dad asked him to play catch.

   _____

   _____

3. Gracie's cousin asked her to come over and play.

   _____

   _____

Challenge: Think about something nice your family has done for you. Write them a thank you note on another sheet of paper.

Name: _____ Date: _____

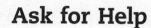

Ask for Help

It can be hard to ask for help. Learning the right way to ask can make a big difference.

Directions: Act out each way to ask your family for help. Find a partner, and act out each part. Or use two toys to act out the scenes yourself. Then, answer the questions.

Part 1: My room is a MESS! If I don't clean it up now, I can't play outside with my brother.

Part 2: Hurry up! I want to play outside.

Part 1: If you help me clean up my room, we can both get outside faster.

Why was this a good way to ask for help?

_____

_____

Part 1: I wish someone would help me make a snack. I wonder what my sister is doing.

Part 2: *(watching TV)*

Part 1: Will you please help me make a snack?

Part 2: I'm just going to watch TV.

Part 1: I can help you clean your room if you help me make a snack.

Why was this a good way to ask for help?

_____

_____

Name: _____ **Date:** _____

Think about What Will Happen Next

Before you do something, think about what might happen next.
That can help you make good choices.

Directions: Draw what might happen next.

1. You stay in your room playing.

3. You clean up and go downstairs.

2. You put the money in your pocket.

4. You bring the money to an adult.

Name: _____ Date: _____

Stand Up for Yourself

Your friends might ask you to do things that you know are not right. You can stand up for yourself and still keep your friends. This is a skill you can practice.

Directions: Write what you should say in each situation to stand up for yourself.

1. Your friend asks you to play a game that you think is unsafe.

_____

_____

2. Your friends are making fun of your clothes.

_____

_____

3. Your friend dares you to steal something from a store.

_____

_____

4. Your friends see a car that is unlocked and tell you to look inside.

_____

_____

Name: _____ Date: _____

Try New Things

Your friends might ask you to do something you have never done before. It can be scary to try new things. It can also be a lot of fun! You might really like it.

Directions: Draw yourself doing each new thing.

1. You are eating dinner with a friend's family. They give you food you have never seen.	**3.** A friend asks you to go on a camping trip. You have never been to this place.
2. A friend asks you to ride a new type of scooter.	**4.** Your friends are all dancing to a song you don't know. They ask you to join.

Focus on Friends

Self-Management

Name: _____ Date: _____

Be Helpful

The way you act can shape how your friends see you. Doing things that help others will let people see you as a helpful friend.

Directions: Circle each person who is being helpful.

Directions: Make a plan to help a friend today.

1. Who will you help? _____

_____

2. What will you do to help? _____

_____

3. How do you think your friend will feel? _____

_____

4. How do you think you will feel? _____

_____

Name: _____ Date: _____

Work Together

You can become better friends with someone when you work together. You learn ways to help your friend. Your friend learns how to help you. You can feel proud of the work you finish as a team.

Directions: Read the story. Then, answer the questions.

Jamar's class is working on a project about animals. Jamar is partners with his best friend, Tonya. She tells Jamar how much she loves foxes and wants to study them. Jamar agrees. He finds a book about foxes. But it's very hard to read. Tonya says she can read it to him. He learns a lot of new facts. Tonya wants to draw the fox, but she can't get it right. Jamar is great at drawing, so he offers to help. They practice sharing their project together. When the time comes, they feel ready.

1. How does Jamar help Tonya?

_____

_____

2. How does Tonya help Jamar?

_____

_____

3. How do you think they felt after they shared with the class?

_____

_____

Name: _____ Date: _____

Think through Your Choices

Stopping to think is *responding*. Acting without thinking is *reacting*. It is better to respond to things with your friends. This helps you make better choices.

Directions: Read each sentence. Write *respond* if the person stopped to think. Write *react* if the person did not stop to think.

1. Mark yells at his friend because he didn't play with him.

   _____

2. Malcolm's feelings are hurt. He talks to his friend about it.

   _____

3. Zayna's friend pushed her, so she tripped her.

   _____

4. Luna's friend is being mean. Luna takes a deep breath and walks away.

   _____

5. Jamie lost a board game with his friends. He asked if they could play again.

   _____

6. Laura's friends decided to play a game she didn't like. She yelled and ran out of the room.

   _____

Benefits of Where You Live

The place where you live can help people. Shelters have warm beds. Schools have teachers. There are many other ways people around you help others.

Directions: Read each sentence. Draw a picture to show who could help.

1. Manny falls down and hurts his arm.

3. Nina wants to play a new sport.

2. Jessica wants to learn to dance.

4. Nathan is hungry.

Name: _____ Date: _____

Cool Down When You Are Angry

You don't always get to choose where you get angry. It can happen at home. It can happen in a public place. Knowing how to cool down can help if you get angry around others.

Directions: How could you calm down? Circle each way that would work for you.

Go for a walk.

Count to 10.

Hug someone.

Find a quiet place to relax.

Be thankful.

Move your body.

Take a breath.

Laugh with someone.

Sit quietly.

Directions: Choose one of these ideas. Draw a picture of you calming down.

Rules Can Be Unfair

People who make rules try to make them fair. This does not always happen.

Directions: Read the stories. Answer the questions.

Luis and June both got caught talking in class. Luis was sent to the principal. June was asked to stop talking.

1. What is unfair?

_____

2. How would you make it more fair?

_____

_____

Jin and Rasheed are playing basketball in a park. They get into a fight and start to yell. The park manager tells Jin that he has to go home. Rasheed gets to stay and play.

3. What is unfair?

_____

4. How would you make it more fair?

_____

_____

Focus on Community

Social Awareness

Name: _____ Date: _____

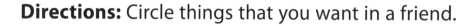

Make Good Friends

It can be hard to find friends. It can be even harder to find good friends. Thinking about what makes a good friend can help you find good friends in your community.

Directions: Circle things that you want in a friend.

kind   smart   silly

funny   loyal   calm

helpful   fair   brave

Directions: Draw something you would like to do with a new friend.

Focus on Community

Relationship Skills

Name: _____ Date: _____

Benefits of Being Thoughtful

Being kind to your neighbors makes them feel good. It can help you feel good, too.

Directions: Write a way to help in each picture.

1.

_____

_____

2.

_____

_____

3.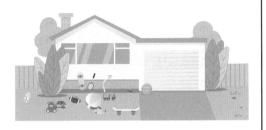

_____

_____

4.

_____

_____

Directions: Helping someone can make you feel proud. Draw how your face looks when you are proud.

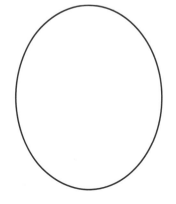

Name: _____ **Date:** _____

See Yourself as a Problem Solver

How you think about yourself is a big deal. If you see yourself as a problem solver, you will be more willing to try to solve problems.

Directions: Write a poem about yourself. Follow the pattern. Write one word to describe you. Then, write two things you can do. Then, choose two things that you will do.

Example

I am *strong*.

I can *help others*.

I can *make people laugh*.

I will *be kind*.

I will *stay calm*.

I am a problem solver!

I am _____.

I can _____.

I can _____.

I will _____.

I will _____.

I am a problem solver!

Directions: Rewrite your poem on a new sheet of paper. Share it with someone.

Name: _____ Date: _____

Be a Problem Solver

Small problems can turn into big ones quickly. You can keep your problems small. But it takes practice.

Directions: Write how you could help each problem stay small.

1. Your friend plays with someone else.

   _____

   _____

2. Two people are talking. You think you hear your name.

   _____

   _____

3. You can't find your favorite shirt.

   _____

   _____

4. Your shoes get dirty at the park.

   _____

   _____

Directions: Color this pledge.

I will be a problem solver!

Name: _____ Date: _____

Focus on Self

Social Awareness

Think about Others' Feelings

It can be hard to have big feelings. But it helps if other people think about how we're feeling. That makes it easier for them to help. You can help other people, too. Think about how they must feel.

Directions: Read each problem. Answer the questions.

Jemma and Erin are at a pool together. Jemma swims really well. She tells Erin to jump in and swim with her. Erin has a hard time swimming. Erin stands by the side of the pool and does not jump in. Jemma tells her it's easy. She tells Erin she just needs to jump.

1. How is Erin feeling? _____

_____

2. What could Jemma say? _____

_____

Milo and Roman are on a soccer team. Milo makes a big mistake and kicks the ball backward toward his own goal. It goes in the goal. Roman is the goalie and didn't stop the ball. Their team loses the game.

3. How is Milo feeling? _____

_____

4. What could Roman say? _____

_____

Name: _____ Date: _____

Outcomes of Conflicts

Problems can end in different ways. Win-Win is when both people get what they want. Win-Lose is when someone gets what they want. That means someone else doesn't get what they want. Lose-Lose is when no one gets what they want.

Directions: Read each problem. Circle how each one ends.

1. Two friends both want to be at the front of the line. They start to argue. So they both get sent to the back of the line.

   win-win   win-lose   lose-lose

2. These two friends both want to play with a basketball. They decide to play a game together.

   win-win   win-lose   lose-lose

3. Two friends are trying to decide who will go first in a game. They play Rock, Paper, Scissors. The winner gets to start.

   win-win   win-lose   lose-lose

Name: _____ Date: _____

Solve Problems for Yourself and Others

Being a problem solver takes work and practice. The more you work at it, the better you will get. Soon, you will be able to help others solve problems, too.

Focus on Self

Responsible Decision-Making

Directions: Read the problem. Answer the questions.

Felix and Tony love playing baseball together. On Sunday, Felix lost control of the ball and hit Tony on the leg. Tony was angry and yelled, "You did that on purpose!"

Felix felt awful. But he didn't like being yelled at. He yelled back, "Don't be a baby!"

1. How is each boy feeling?

Felix: _____

Tony: _____

2. How can they solve the problem?

_____

3. Draw your solution to the problem.

_____

4. What type of solution is this? (Circle one.)

Win-Win   Win-Lose   Lose-Lose

Name: _____ Date: _____

Know How You Feel

There are many words for feelings. They are all different, but some are related. It's good to have a lot of words to explain how you feel. This can help you be a better neighbor.

Directions: Put each of the feelings from the Word Bank into the right group.

Mad	Happy	Sad	Shy

Word Bank

angry	excited	gloomy	silly
blue	fearful	nervous	unhappy
cheerful	furious	scared	upset

Directions: Choose one of these words. Draw what your face looks like when you feel that way.

Name: _____ Date: _____

Calming Down

It is normal to have conflicts while you are playing in your neighborhood. This can lead to big feelings. It helps to take a pause or a quick break to help your body stay calm.

Directions: People take breaks in a lot of ways. Study the pictures. Write how each person is taking a break.

1. _____

_____

2. _____

_____

Directions: Draw a picture of how you take a break.

Focus on Neighborhood

Self-Management

Name: _____ Date: _____

Predict Your Friends' Feelings

To predict is to make a good guess about what might happen next. It can help you make good choices. You can also avoid doing things that hurt your friends' feelings. You can choose to do things that might help people feel better.

Directions: Imagine you find $10 on the ground at school. Complete the chart. Then, answer the questions.

You keep the money.	You turn the money in at the office.
How would you feel? _____ _____	How would you feel? _____ _____
How would the person who lost the money feel? _____ _____	How would the person who lost the money feel? _____ _____

1. How would you feel if you lost money and did not get it back?

   _____

2. How would you feel if you lost money and did get it back?

   _____

Name: _____ Date: _____

Be Strong

Your neighborhood has people who stand up for what is right. They speak up when they see things that are unfair. They say something when people are treated differently. These people are brave. They are also strong.

Directions: Think about the good things people do in your neighborhood. How do they stand up for each other? How do they help each other? Write as many good things as you can think of in the person.

Feel Good about Your Choices

When you make good choices, your neighborhood is safer. Good choices help you stay safe, too. Good choices can make you feel better about yourself.

Directions: Read these true stories of neighborhood heroes. Answer the questions.

The Drawer is a group started by some neighbors. They gather socks for people who don't have any. Then, they give the socks away.

1. How might people feel after getting new socks?

_____

2. How would it feel to give socks to a person who needs them?

_____

Toys for Tots raises money to buy toys. They give them to kids whose families can't afford them. They also collect toys to give to kids.

3. How does Toys for Tots make other people feel?

_____

4. How would it feel to give a toy to a kid who didn't have one?

_____

Focus on Neighborhood
Responsible Decision-Making

Name: _____ Date: _____

Reflect

To reflect is to think about how you feel. It also means to think about the things you do. This helps you change and get better. It is helpful to reflect at school.

Directions: Find a piece of schoolwork you did in the last few days. Then, answer the questions about it. This is one way to reflect.

1. What work did you choose?_____

   _____

2. What did you learn?_____

   _____

3. Did you do your best?_____

   _____

4. What could you have done better?_____

   _____

5. What questions will you ask yourself next time?

   _____

   _____

   _____

Name: _____ Date: _____

Improve Yourself

It's good to push yourself to do better. You can do that by practicing. Think about what kind of practice will help you most.

Directions: Write what you think each person could do to get better.

1. Kelly missed 10 words on her spelling test.

_____

_____

2. Kenai adds every time he sees the subtraction sign.

_____

_____

3. Sasha's teacher says she can't read Sasha's handwriting.

_____

_____

4. Jon wants to learn how to skateboard.

_____

_____

Name: _____ Date: _____

Find What Others Are Good At

It can help to work with a friend when you are trying to get better. Find a friend who is really good at what you want to improve. Then, ask for their help.

Directions: Find a puppet, stuffed animals, or a friend. Act out the scene below.

Puppet 1: I am never going to remember my math facts.

Puppet 2: 2 + 2 is 4. 4 + 4 is 8. 8 + 8 is 16.

Puppet 1: I should ask for some help. Who is really good at math?

Puppet 2: 3 + 3 is 6. 6 + 6 is 12. 12 + 12 is 24.

Puppet 1: Hey, I see that you are really good at math. Can you help me remember my facts?

Puppet 2: Sure! I like to make up patterns when I add. It helps me remember. I do simple doubles facts to start off.

Puppet 1: Ok, so 1 + 1 is easy. That is 2.

Puppet 2: Now, do 2 + 2.

Puppet 1: That is 4! I know that one!

Puppet 2: Now, try 4 + 4.

Puppet 1: That is harder. I'll start at 4 and count up. So 5, 6, 7, 8. It's 8!

Puppet 2: That is right! Now, do it again. When you do it over and over, your brain will remember it!

Puppet 1: Thank you so much for helping me.

Focus on School

Social Awareness

Name: _____ **Date:** _____

Teamwork

Working as a team can be rewarding. It also takes a lot of work and planning. One way to make sure teamwork goes well is to make sure everyone does their own job. This makes the work go smoothly. It can even make the work go quickly.

Directions: Circle three things that are part of good teamwork. Put a star next to the one you think is most important.

Take turns.   Manage time well.

Stay focused.   Be kind.

Be a problem solver. Have fun.

Listen to each other. Voice your ideas.

Directions: Think about the item that you starred. Draw a picture of what it looks like to you.

Name: _____   Date: _____

Responsible Decision-Making

Make Good Choices

We all make mistakes. But if you think about your mistakes, you can learn from them. You can grow and stop making the same mistakes.

Directions: These children each made a mistake. They do not want to make the mistake again. Write what they could do next time.

1. This girl was supposed to use a learning app. She clicked on a game instead.

   _____

   _____

2. This boy is upset about losing a game and threw the game board.

   _____

   _____

3. This boy made fun of a friend for not doing well on a math test.

   _____

   _____

4. This girl pushed three other kids to get to the front of the lunch line.

   _____

   _____

Name: _____ **Date:** _____

Be Mindful

Communities can be busy. They can also be noisy. It helps to stop. Give yourself a minute to look and to listen. You can be more connected to a place if you see and hear what is around you. This is called being *mindful*.

Directions: Work through each step. This will help you be more mindful. Then, answer the questions.

Step 1: Be still. Lie down if you can. Or just sit quietly.

Step 2: Relax your arms. Turn your palms out.

Step 3: Close your eyes.

Step 4: Listen to any sounds you can hear. Try to listen to each one by itself. Name what you think each sound is. For example, if you hear people talking, say to yourself *people talking*.

Step 5: Breathe in through your nose as you count to 5. Breathe out through your mouth as you count to 8. Do this slowly seven times. Focus on each breath as you count.

Step 6. Open your eyes.

1. How do you feel?

   _____

   _____

2. When could it help to do this exercise on your own?

   _____

   _____

Name: _____ **Date:** _____

Focus on Community

Self-Management

Stress Management

Think about how it feels to be upset. Using self-talk can help you control your stress. It can help you calm down.

Directions: Match which self-talk would go with each stressful moment. Then, color the self-talk that you will try to use soon.

You spill juice on your favorite shirt.

I really wanted to see that movie. I know I can see it another time.

You are at a fair, and your favorite ride is broken.

I am so bummed. But there are other rides I enjoy.

You are going to a movie at the theater. When you get there, the movie is sold out.

I really wanted to try one. I'll ask my sister if she can make some more.

You are excited to try the cookies your big sister made. They are all gone before you get one.

I love this shirt. I can try to get the stain out when I get home.

Name: _____ **Date:** _____

Be Thankful

Life can be hard. But trying to find something good can help.
When something bad happens, stop and think about where the
good is.

Directions: Write something that each person could be thankful for.

1. Juan is at a community center. None of the basketball courts
are free. The pool is open.

_____

_____

2. Darla is going to a toy store to spend her birthday money. The
toy she wanted is not there.

_____

_____

3. Jessica is on a sports team. She loses her first game.

_____

_____

4. Roman is playing at a park and wants to swing. Every swing
is taken.

_____

_____

Name: _____ Date: _____

Make Good Friends

Talking with a friend can help when you feel stressed. Doing things with people you care about can also help you feel relaxed.

Directions: These are things you can do in your community. Many of them are better with friends. Write an idea of your own. Then, put a star by one you would like to do with a friend.

Go on a walk.	Get some ice cream.
Ride bikes.	Go to a mall.
Go to a movie.	Play a game.
Go swimming.	Your idea: _____

Directions: Draw you and a friend doing the activity you starred.

Name: _____   Date: _____

Help Your Community

You can help other people stay calm. The best thing you can do is to stay calm. This a very powerful tool. It can help your community stay safe.

Directions: Read the stories about people who helped others. Answer the questions.

Martin Luther King Jr. stood up for people's rights. He wanted Black people to be treated the same as white people. He spoke up about laws that were unfair. Laws changed because of what he did.

1. What was one thing King did to help his community?

_____

2. How is King a good example?_____

_____

Susan B. Anthony lived at a time when women were not allowed to vote. She thought this was unfair. She protested. She gave speeches. She did not live to see things change. But in 1920, women were finally allowed to vote.

3. What is one thing Anthony did to help her community?

_____

4. How is Anthony a good example?_____

_____

Name: _____ Date: _____

Focus on Self

Self-Awareness

Know the Size of Problems

Problems are easier to solve when you know how big they are. Figure out if a problem is small, medium, or big. Then, you can work to fix it. A small problem is one you fix on your own. A medium problem is one that you can solve with help. A big problem always needs an adult.

Directions: Circle the size of each problem.

1. You are getting ready to go outside. You can't find one of your shoes.

    small   medium   big

2. You are jumping on your bed. You fall off and hurt your arm.

    small   medium   big

3. Your mom makes you a sandwich you do not like for lunch.

    small   medium   big

4. You left your backpack at school.

    small   medium   big

5. You see two kids bullying someone at recess.

    small   medium   big

6. You can't find your notebook in your desk.

    small   medium   big

Name: _____ Date: _____

Solve Small Problems on Your Own

You can solve small problems on your own. It is very brave to try to solve your own problems.

Directions: Write how you would solve each small problem.

1. You make a mistake on your homework. You can't find an eraser.

   _____

2. Someone bumps into you in the hallway. You drop a book.

   _____

3. You are reading aloud to your class. You say a word wrong.

   _____

4. There is a long line at the slide.

   _____

5. You don't get to go to your friend's house.

   _____

6. The apple in your lunch is bruised.

   _____

Self-Management

Focus on Self

Name: _____ Date: _____

Solve Medium Problems with Others

Medium problems can be solved with a little help. It can take some work to solve these problems. But it's always worth it.

Focus on Self

Social Awareness

Directions: Study the pictures. Write how you would solve each problem with someone else.

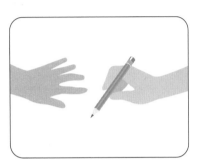

You need a pencil to finish your work.

1. Who would you ask for help?

_____

2. How would you solve the problem?

_____

_____

_____

You rip a page in a library book.

3. Who would you ask for help?

_____

4. How would you solve the problem?

_____

_____

5. Who would you ask for help?

_____

6. How would you solve the problem?

_____

Water leaked into your backpack.

_____

Name: _____ Date: _____

Solving Problems with Friends

There are a lot of good things about solving problems with friends. It makes it easier to solve the problems. It can also help you be a better friend.

Directions: Color the boxes that are good ways to solve problems with friends. Write an *X* on the boxes that are not.

Close your eyes.	Ask for help.	Push someone.	Throw something.
Use positive self-talk.	Think of another way.	Count down from 10.	Stay calm.
Stop and think.	Hide in your room.	Steal something.	Yell.
Ask for a break.	Call someone a name.	Take a deep breath.	Give up.
Get an adult.	Talk about your choices.	Make a mean face.	Say, "I can do this!"

Directions: Read the text. Choose one of the ways to solve a problem from the chart. Write how you would use it to solve this problem.

You and a friend are playing in your neighborhood. The ball you are playing with gets stuck in a tree. It is too high to reach.

_____

_____

Relationship Skills

Focus on Self

Name: _____   Date:_____

Respond to Problems

Not every problem needs the same type of response. A small problem does not need a big response. A big problem does not need a small response.

Directions: Decide whether each response matches the problem.

Problems

| You do not have any milk for your cereal. | You knock down your building block creation. It breaks apart. | Your TV is not working. |

↓   ↓   ↓

Reactions

| You throw the bowl of cereal onto the floor. | You take a deep breath and then start rebuilding. | You throw the remote against the wall. |

Do they match?

| yes   no | yes   no | yes   no |

Directions: Write a reaction that matches this problem.

Your family serves a dinner that you do not like.

_____

_____

Name: _____ Date: _____

Connect Your Feelings to Your Behavior

Your feelings are connected to your actions. The way you feel can change how you act. Checking in with your feelings can help shape how you act. It can also help when you are doing hard things.

Directions: Look at how each person is acting. Write how you think they are feeling. On another sheet of paper, draw how you would act if someone gave you a present.

1. _____

3. _____

2. _____

4. _____

Focus on Family

Self-Awareness

Name: _____ **Date:** _____

Control Your Behavior

Thinking you can do something is a big first step. If you think you can do something, then you are more likely to do it.

Directions: Read each story. Answer the questions.

Carla thinks she is bad at drawing. She does not think the lines on her paper match what she sees in her head. Carla has art class on the first day of second grade.

1. How do you think Carla feels in class?

_____

2. How do you think art class will go?

_____

_____

Leroy loves playing baseball with his dad. He practices for weeks. He goes to a tryout for a baseball team.

3. How do you think Leroy feels at the tryout?

_____

4. How do you think the tryout will go?

_____

_____

Name: _____ **Date:** _____

Show Concern for Others' Feelings

Take time to think about how your friends and family feel. This will help show how much you care about them.

Directions: Read the texts. Answer the questions.

> Leann dropped her favorite drinking glass. It broke.
>
> **1.** How do you think Leann is feeling?
>
> _____
>
> **2.** Draw a nice thing you could do to help.

> Ramone was in the car when it crashed. He is okay, but he was scared.
>
> **3.** How do you think Ramone is feeling?
>
> _____
>
> **4.** Draw a nice thing you could do to help.

Name: _____ Date: _____

Focus on Family

Relationship Skills

Offer Help to Your Family

It is good to help your family when they need it. This can help you feel closer to them. It will also help you feel happy.

Directions: Write a short story about how each person is helping.

1. Gloria helps her sister.

_____

_____

_____

2. Leon helps his stepmom.

_____

_____

_____

Directions: Draw a picture to go with one of your stories.

126958—180 Days of Social-Emotional Learning

© Shell Education

Name: _____ **Date:** _____

Your Family Impacts Your Thinking

Your family has its own way of thinking and doing things. What they think and do can shape how you think and feel.

Directions: Think about your family. Answer the questions.

My family likes to _____ for fun.

My family doesn't like to _____.

My family shows we love each other by _____

_____.

Focus on Family

Responsible Decision-Making

Directions: Draw a special thing your family does.

Name: _____   Date: _____

I-Messages

An *I-message* is a way to say how you feel. It is called this because it begins with *I*. I-messages can help solve problems. They help you focus on your feelings.

Directions: Write how each person feels. Complete each I-message.

Jerome and Larry are coloring. Larry took Jerome's box of crayons.

Jerome feels _____.

Jerome can say, "When you take my crayons, I feel

_____."

Kat and Angel are playing outside. Angel ran by Kat and bumped her.

Kat feels _____.

Kat can say, "When you bumped into me, I felt

_____."

Ivy and Wendel are talking. Ivy is telling a story. Wendel cuts her off. He starts to tell his own story.

Ivy feels _____.

Ivy can say, "When you interrupt me, I feel

_____."

Focus on Friends **Self-Awareness**

Name: _____ Date: _____

I-Messages

I-messages can help you sort out why something bothers you. This is the *when* part of an I-message.

Directions: Help Lee complete his I-message. Then, answer the questions.

Lee and Izzy are reading a book together. Izzy won't share the book. Lee can't see it very well.

Lee feels annoyed.

Lee's I-message: *I feel annoyed when Izzy* _____

_____

1. What is something a friend does that bothers you?

_____

2. When does it happen?

_____

3. Write an I-message about it.

I feel _____ when _____

_____.

Next time, will you please _____

_____?

Name: _____ Date: _____

Focus on Friends

Social Awareness

I-Messages

An I-message is one way to solve a problem. It can help you think about how someone feels. This is called *empathy*. It is a great first step in problem solving.

Directions: Read each conflict. Write how each person might be feeling.

Kyle and Erin are riding bikes. Kyle loses control of his bike. He runs into Erin, and she falls off. Both of them scrape their knees. They start to argue.

1. How is Erin feeling? _____

_____

2. How is Kyle feeling? _____

_____

Luke and Rocky are running a race. Rocky barely wins. Luke yells that he thinks Rocky cheated.

3. How is Luke feeling? _____

_____

4. How is Rocky feeling? _____

_____

WEEK 19
DAY
4

Name: _____ Date: _____

I-Messages

An I-message helps you solve problems. When you use an I-message, you have to use a strong voice. Don't yell, but don't whisper either. Speak with confidence.

Directions: Write what is wrong with each I-message. Then, write a better I-message for either Justin or Vivi.

1. Justin yelled to Stephanie, "You stole my snack! I am so mad! Next time, I will knock you down!"

   What did Justin do wrong?

   _____

   _____

2. Vivi whispers to Dave, "Umm, I kind of feel maybe a little annoyed. Because, you know, you tripped me. And I fell down. Next time, maybe slow down little?"

   What did Vivi do wrong?

   _____

   _____

3. _____

   _____

Name: _____ Date: _____

Focus on Friends

Responsible Decision-Making

I-Messages

I-messages do not always work. They work well with people you know. If you do not know a person, an I-message might not work.

Directions: Circle whether each person should use an I-message.

1. Ronnie and Josh just met at camp. Ronnie wanted a bed by his friend. He moved Josh's bag to a different bed.

   yes   no

2. Leo and his best friend Ryan are playing catch. Ryan ran away with the ball.

   yes   no

3. Erin and Andrew have been friends for a long time. Erin took Andrew's skateboard. She did not ask first.

   yes   no

4. Malia is Leslie's new friend at school. Leslie asked Malia to come to her house. While there, Malia broke one of Leslie's toys.

   yes   no

Directions: Choose one person from these examples who should use an I-message. Write what they could say.

I feel _____ when _____

_____

Next time, will you please _____

_____ ?

Name: _____ Date: _____

Know How You Feel

Your community is full of things to do. Some of them may be new to you. Sometimes, it can be hard to try new things. You may feel embarrassed. Other times, you try something new that you are good at, and you feel proud.

Directions: Write whether each activity is easy or hard for you. Then, draw a face to show how you feel about it.

1. swimming	Is this easy or hard? _____	
2. drawing	Is this easy or hard? _____	
3. running	Is this easy or hard? _____	
4. reading	Is this easy or hard? _____	
5. making new friends	Is this easy or hard? _____	
6. dancing	Is this easy or hard? _____	

Focus on Community

Self-Awareness

Name: _____   Date: _____

Ask for Help

When something is hard, you may want to quit. But if you practice, you will likely get better. You can also ask for help from someone who is an expert. They can give you tips and teach you.

Directions: Read the new thing each person wants to try. Write an expert who could help them.

1. Molly wants to learn more about wildflowers.

   _____

2. Ezra is having a hard time learning to swim.

   _____

3. Maria wants to learn about what a nurse does.

   _____

4. Nate would like to get better at drawing.

   _____

Directions: What is something you would like to learn? Draw yourself asking an expert for help.

Name: _____ Date: _____

Find Others' Strengths

People can win awards. But places in a community can win, too. There are awards for the best place to eat, the best place to play, and even the best schools.

Directions: Read the list of awards. Which places in your community should win?

Best Place to Eat: _____

Best Park: _____

Best Place to Get a Toy: _____

Best Place to Get a Snack: _____

Best Place to Have Fun: _____

Directions: Draw a place you think should win an award.

Focus on Community

Social Awareness

Name: _____ Date: _____

Skills for Being a Leader

Your community is full of leaders. Leadership takes a lot of skills.
Leaders have to listen well. They have to help people. They have
to set good examples.

Directions: Circle the things that make a good leader. Answer
the question.

cares about others

able to set goals   reliable

loud talker

good singer   tall

good listener

positive   creative

good at sports

funny   good cook

strong

helpful   trustworthy

dresses well

1. What leadership skills do you have?

_____

_____

_____

Name: _____ Date: _____

Solve Problems

Every community has problems. Leaders help solve them. This takes a lot of hard work. It also takes a lot of creativity.

Directions: This community needs help solving problems. Write what you think they should do.

1. A park starts to fill with trash. No one is cleaning it up.

_____

_____

2. A community building is old and run-down. The roof leaks. Walls are starting to fall down.

_____

_____

3. Many families do not have a place to sleep.

_____

_____

4. There are a lot of car crashes at a certain corner.

_____

_____

Name: _____ Date: _____

Be Honest

Using computers can be a lot of fun. It can also be dangerous. Adults set rules for how to use computers. They do that to make sure you stay safe. Part of being honest is following those rules.

Directions: Read the rules. Then, draw your favorite thing to do on the computer.

Use two hands when carrying a computer.

Don't eat food or drink anything near a computer.

Stay focused.

Press keys lightly.

Do not use someone else's password.

Do not open programs you are not allowed to use.

Do not message anyone without permission.

Charge your device when you are done using it.

Name: _____ **Date:** _____

Ask for Help

Things can go wrong when you are using a computer. Sometimes, you need to ask for help right away.

Directions: Circle the things that you would need help with.

You drop your device. The screen cracks.

Your device is almost out of power.

You forgot your password.

Your app crashes. You can't get it to open again.

You lose a game you are playing.

An ad pops up.

Directions: Choose one thing you circled. Complete the sentence. Then, draw yourself asking for help.

Can you please help me _____?

Self-Management Focus on Self

Name: _____   Date: _____

Focus on Self
Social Awareness

Be Kind to Others

Some games and programs let you talk to your friends online. Some let you talk to people you do not know. It is important to be kind with your words, no matter where you are. It is also important to be safe.

Directions: Match the statement with the kind words that go with it.

Someone beats you in a game.	Delete and ignore messages from strangers.
Your friend hurts your feelings.	"Nice game. Let's play again."
Someone you do not know tries to message you.	"What you said really hurt my feelings."

Directions: Draw a comic of one of these scenes.

126958—180 Days of Social-Emotional Learning   © Shell Education

Name: _____ **Date:** _____

Digital Communication

It can be hard to say what you mean when you type a message. Your friend can't see your face or hear your voice. You need to make sure your message is read the way you want it to be.

Directions: Read each set of statements. Answer the questions to compare them.

1. "I want to talk to you."   "I WANT TO TALK TO YOU!"
   How are they alike?

   _____

   How are they different?

   _____

2. "I want to hang out with you."   "I will not hang out with you."
   How are they alike?

   _____

   How are they different?

   _____

3. "You are my best friend."   "We're BFFs."
   How are they alike?

   _____

   How are they different?

   _____

Name: _____ Date: _____

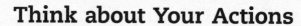

Think about Your Actions

What you do matters. This is true on devices, too. When you treat your devices with respect, you likely won't have problems. When you treat them poorly, problems can happen.

Directions: Write what could happen in each example.

1. Your grandma lets you play a game for 30 minutes. She is not paying attention. You play for an extra 20 minutes.

   _____

   _____

2. You open a device at school. The person before you did not log out. They have 1,000 gold coins in a game. You decide to spend all of them.

   _____

   _____

3. You meant to save your work. You pressed the print button instead. It starts to print 20 pages.

   _____

   _____

4. You are drinking water near a laptop. Your arm knocks the water onto the keyboard.

   _____

   _____

Name: _____ **Date:** _____

Examine Bias

People are more alike than we are different. It is easier to see the things that are different. Sometimes, those things are scary. Try to remember that we are mostly the same. That can help you feel less scared.

Directions: Think of a person in your neighborhood. Draw them in the first box. Draw yourself in the second box. Then, answer the questions.

Focus on Neighborhood

Self-Awareness

┌─────────────────────┐ ┌─────────────────────┐
│   │ │   │
│   │ │   │
│   │ │   │
└─────────────────────┘ └─────────────────────┘

1. What is the person's name?

_____

2. How do you and the person look the same?

_____

3. How do you look different?

_____

4. What does the person like to do for fun?

_____

5. Do you like to do any of the same things?

_____

Name: _____ Date: _____

Focus on Neighborhood

Self-Management

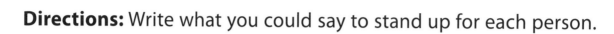

Stand Up for Others

Sometimes, people are teased for being different. Standing up for them is the right thing to do. It will make you feel good. It will also help build a strong neighborhood.

Directions: Write what you could say to stand up for each person.

1. Daniel wears glasses. Kids in your neighborhood tease him about it.

   _____

   _____

2. Jorge was born with a leg that doesn't work very well. He uses crutches to walk. Kids in your neighborhood tease him about it. They pretend to walk like they need crutches, too.

   _____

   _____

3. Lizzy is shorter than other kids. Some people think she is younger. Kids in your neighborhood tease her about it.

   _____

   _____

4. Kiera dresses differently. She wears a different type of clothes. Kids in your neighborhood tease her about it.

   _____

   _____

Name: _____ Date: _____

Think about Others' Feelings

People in your neighborhood might think in a different way. They might live in a different way, too. We are all different. This is a good thing! We just need to think about each other.

Directions: Read each example. Write how each person might be feeling.

Mr. Nelson is an older man in your neighborhood. He doesn't go outside often. Some kids like to ring his doorbell and then run away.

_____

David loves to dance. But people stare at him in class. He hears people laughing as he leaves. After he told his friends about dance class, they stopped asking him to play basketball.

_____

Amy has dreamed of being a pro football player. She practices with her friends every day. She trains hard. She works out. She watches games with her family every week. Then, she is told that she can't play because she is a girl.

_____

Focus on Neighborhood

Social Awareness

Name: _____   Date: _____

Focus on Neighborhood

Relationship skills

Offer to Help Others

An ally is a person who stands up for others. It takes strength to do that. It is brave to try to help other people.

Directions: Draw a line from the problem to the words you could use to help.

A group of friends sees a person at the park with a dirty shirt. They start to tease him.

"Hey, it's not nice to laugh at people. It was just a mistake. It could happen to any of us."

A teammate on your basketball team slips and the ball goes out of bounds. Your team laughs at him.

"That is not cool! You shouldn't make fun of people. He might be having a bad day."

A friend tells a group of neighbors that he has to go home for dinner. They start to tease him. They call him a baby.

"It's no big deal! She is just trying to do what her parents told her. Let's go do something we all can do."

A group of neighbors is going to play a video game together. One person says she is not allowed to play that game. The group starts to tease her.

"Come on, he is just eating with his family. Lay off of him."

Name: _____ Date: _____

Saying Sorry

Being able to say sorry takes practice. It can be hard to admit when you are wrong. It can be embarrassing, too. But you'll feel better after you do.

Directions: Read each example. Fill in the letter for the best apology.

1. You are playing baseball in your neighborhood. You lose control of the ball. It breaks the window of a car.

   Ⓐ "I'm sorry I broke your window. I lost control of the ball. Is there anything I can do to help make this better?"

   Ⓑ "Sorry your window broke. But it wasn't my fault. My friend was making faces at me."

2. You borrowed your neighbor's tennis ball. You dropped it, and it rolled down the storm drain. Now, it is gone.

   Ⓐ "Sorry I lost your ball. But you lose my stuff all the time! It's no big deal."

   Ⓑ "I'm sorry I lost your ball. Can I give you one of mine to make up for it?"

Directions: Read the example. Write an apology.

You are playing in a neighbor's yard. You forget to close the gate. Their dog gets out and runs away.

_____

_____

Name: _____ Date: _____

Focus on School

Self-Awareness

Know How You Feel

You can have a lot of feelings in one school day. One of the biggest feelings is anger. There are a lot of levels of anger. Knowing how they are different can help you feel less angry.

Directions: These words are all a type of anger. Sort the words from most to least angry. Put the word that means the least angry on the bottom. Put the word that means the most angry on the top.

Anger Words	
annoyed	mad
frustrated	outraged
fuming	rage
irritated	upset

_____

_____

_____

_____

_____

_____

_____

_____

Directions: Choose one of these anger words. Write about a time at school when you felt this way. Write what you did to feel less angry.

_____

_____

_____

Name: _____ Date: _____

Control Your Body

When your body gets angry at school, it can be hard to know what to do. But if you have a plan, you will more likely stay safe.

Directions: Look at where you are learning right now. Draw your space. Include tables, chairs, and other objects. Then, follow the steps to add more to your drawing.

1. Taking a break away from others can help you calm down. Circle a place where you could go to take a break.

2. Talking to other people helps, too. Put a square around a place where you could go talk to someone.

3. Drinking water can also help. Put a triangle around where you could find water.

4. Stopping to breathe is another way to cool down. Draw yourself taking a deep breath.

5. Moving your body also helps with anger. Draw a friend doing jumping jacks.

Name: _____ Date: _____

Focus on School

Social Awareness

Help Others Calm Down

Your friends will get angry at school, just like you do. You can find ways to help them manage their anger.

Directions: Write what you could say to help a friend in each example. Then, draw what you could do.

1. Your friend failed a math test.

_____

_____

3. Your friend can't find the right marker in art class. He rips up his page.

_____

_____

2. Your friend was not invited to a birthday party.

_____

_____

4. Someone pushes your friend at recess. She stops playing and sits down.

_____

_____

Solve Conflicts

Your friends will make you angry. You will make them angry. Solving conflicts when someone is angry can be hard work. But it's worth it.

Directions: Read each of the conflicts. Act out solving them with a friend or stuffed animals.

> Your best friend trips on a chair and falls down. You start to laugh. Your friend gets angry.
>
> **You:** I'm sorry I laughed at you when you fell. Are you okay? Is there anything I can do to help?

> A kid walks by you at lunch and says that your lunch smells funny. You are mad.
>
> **You:** Did you hear that?
>
> **Friend:** Yeah, that was really mean!
>
> **You:** That person must be having a bad day.

Directions: Read the conflict. Write what you could say to your friend when the lesson is over.

Your friend starts talking to you during a reading lesson. Your teacher thinks it's you and tells you to stop talking. You get embarrassed and are annoyed by your friend.

_____

_____

_____

Name: _____ Date: _____

Focus on School

Responsible Decision-Making

Big and Small Conflicts

There will always be times when you are angry. When the problem is small, you can solve it on your own. But some problems will be bigger. You may need some help solving them.

Directions: Decide which problems are big and which are small. Write *big* in the boxes with big problems. Write *small* in the boxes with small problems.

1. You can't find your pencil. The teacher has started the lesson. _____	**5.** You lose a game during P.E. _____
2. Your friend hits you really hard on the playground. _____	**6.** You don't feel like being with the group in music. _____
3. You lost your math book. _____	**7.** You rip a page while you are erasing a mistake. _____
4. Your friend is teasing you about your new shoes. _____	**8.** You are playing tag. A friend pushes you down, and you hurt your arm. _____

Name: _____ **Date:** _____

Connect Feelings to Actions

It is helpful to know what makes you happy. It is also helpful to know what makes you sad. If you understand your feelings, you can learn more about them. This can bring you more joy. It can also help you avoid things that make you upset.

Directions: Read the list of activities. Check the ones that bring you joy.

☐ going to the library   ☐ eating out

☐ riding a bike   ☐ shopping

☐ singing   ☐ playing video games

☐ cheering for a sports team   ☐ going to a park

☐ playing outside   ☐ reading

Directions: Think about a time you did one of these things. Write about how you felt. Draw yourself doing the activity.

_____

_____

_____

_____

_____

Focus on Community

Self-Awareness

Name: _____ Date: _____

Find Your Triggers

A trigger is something that makes you upset. Triggers make you feel upset quickly. They seem to come out of nowhere. You can manage a lot of big feelings if you know your triggers. You can prepare with self-talk. You can calm down quickly. You can also avoid the traps that make you upset.

Directions: Circle the things that trigger you.

Someone is being mean to other people.

A person throws a fit about losing a game.

Someone says mean things about your family.

People are doing things you can't.

A person has nicer things than you.

People touch your things without asking.

People make fun of you.

Someone doesn't get in trouble for doing something mean.

Someone cuts in line.

Someone yells at you.

Someone takes something you are using.

Directions: Choose one of your triggers. Write how you would control your anger. Choose to use self-talk, taking a break, or talking about it.

_____

_____

_____

_____

Name: _____ Date: _____

Show Concern for Others' Feelings

People in your community have triggers of their own. Theirs might be different than yours. It can be confusing when people get mad and you do not know why. Giving people space will help. It can keep small problems small.

Directions: Write what each person's trigger might be.

1. Claire was playing softball. She swung and missed the ball for strike 3. She was mad and threw her helmet on the ground.

_____

2. Keisha was at the store. Her family was checking out, and a man cut in front of them. She stomped her feet and yelled to her mom that it was unfair.

_____

3. Ronald was walking on a trail with his dad. He got mud on his new boots. He was so mad, he threw a stick into the woods and yelled.

_____

4. Keefer was at the library. He saw someone putting books into a bag without checking them out. He was fuming and went to tell the librarian.

_____

Focus on Community
Social Awareness

Name: _____ **Date:** _____

Stand Up for Others

A common trigger is unfairness. No one likes to be treated unfairly. If you see someone being treated that way, it is good to speak up. It is also very brave. One of the best ways to make a community strong is to stand up for others.

Directions: Not every family has enough food. This may seem unfair. Write why it is important that all people have food. Then, draw what your community could do to help.

_____

_____

_____

Name: _____ Date: _____

Think about How You Can Help

You can make a change. You can make a difference. Kids in second grade have chances to make their communities better.

Directions: Read the list of ways to volunteer. Write your own idea. Then, circle one that you could do.

1. Visit a nursing home, and play games with an older person.

2. Buy a toy for someone who can't afford one.

3. Clean up a park or your school playground.

4. Make cookies and thank you cards for police officers or firefighters.

5. Join a run or race to support people's health.

6. Give a box of games to kids in the hospital.

7. Spend time at an animal shelter.

8. _____

Directions: Draw yourself doing the activity you chose.

Name: _____   Date: _____

Focus on Self

Self-Awareness

Think Positively

Your brain is like a muscle. It works just like the muscles that help your body move. You can work out to get stronger arms. You can also work out your brain! Using affirmations, or positive thoughts, is one way to make your brain stronger.

Directions: Read these affirmations. Circle three you could say every day.

Today will be great.   Today is a new day.

I will make good choices today.   I can get through anything.

I can do anything.   I matter.

I've got this.   I am ready to learn.

I choose my mood.   I am smart.

I will be positive.   People like me for who I am.

I will do my best.   I will ask questions to grow today.

Everything will be okay.   My best is enough.

Directions: Write the three you chose. Say each one three times a day for a week.

1. _____

2. _____

3. _____

Name: _____ **Date:** _____

Helping Others Helps You

Helping others can help you feel good, too.

Directions: Write things that could help your friends or family.

I can help others by…

_____

_____

I can help others by…

_____

I can help others by…

_____

_____

I can help others by…

_____

_____

Directions: Answer how you can help someone today.

1. Who do you want to help?

_____

2. How can you help them?

_____

_____

Focus on Self

Self-Management

Name: _____   Date: _____

Focus on Self

Social Awareness

Affirmations for Others

Giving a kind note is a nice thing to do. It makes someone feel really good when you think of them. A note with a positive message can mean a lot.

Directions: Read the list of affirmations. Circle three you could write to someone else. Then, follow the steps.

Today will be great.	You will make good choices today.	You can do anything.	You've got this.
You get better every day.	Everything will be okay.	Today is a new day.	You will do your best.
You matter.	You are ready to learn.	You are an amazing person.	You can get through anything.
People like you for who you are.	You will make a difference.	Your best is enough.	You are smart.

1. Write one of the affirmations you circled.

_____

_____

2. Write the name of someone you could give this affirmation to.

_____

Name: _____ Date: _____

Ask Questions

Ask your friends good questions. This will help you learn a lot about them.

Directions: Ask a friend each question. Draw their answers.

1. What is your favorite thing to do for fun?

2. Would you rather be able to fly or walk through walls? Why?

3. What is your favorite TV show?

Name: _____ Date: _____

Focus on Self

Responsible Decision-Making

Think through Your Choices

An impulse is a thing you want to do right now. Impulses can lead to bad choices. You can control impulses by thinking about your choices.

Directions: Read each example. Then, read the three choices. Fill in the letter for the best choice.

1. You are playing a game with your friend. He says something mean.

   Ⓐ Let your friend know that he hurt your feelings.

   Ⓑ Say something mean back.

   Ⓒ Punch him in the arm.

2. You are working on some homework. You can't solve one question.

   Ⓐ Sit and wait.

   Ⓑ Ask someone for help.

   Ⓒ Rip up your paper.

3. You are playing your favorite game. You are told to shut it off to eat dinner.

   Ⓐ Don't listen and keep playing.

   Ⓑ Throw the controller down, and yell that it's not fair.

   Ⓒ Shut it off, and go to the table for dinner.

Name: _____ Date: _____

Deal with Disappointment

There are times when you really want something but don't get it. That feeling is called *disappointment*. It can be hard when you don't get what you want.

Directions: Look at each picture. Write why each person might be disappointed. Then, write the self-talk they could use to feel better.

1. Disappointment: _____

_____

Self-Talk: _____

_____

2. Disappointment: _____

_____

Self-Talk: _____

_____

3. Disappointment: _____

_____

Self-Talk: _____

_____

Name: _____ Date: _____

Focus on Family

Self-Management

Self-Control

It can be hard to stop yourself when you really want to do something. That strong feeling is called an *impulse*. It can burst like a volcano and spill out. Or it can freeze like an iceberg. If you can learn to freeze an impulse, you can make better choices.

Directions: Read each story. Write what the volcano reaction would be. Then, write what the iceberg reaction would be. Follow the example.

Example: Your friend is talking about a soccer game they played. You also played soccer. You scored the winning goal!

Volcano: Yell, "I won the game for my team."

Iceberg: Wait until my friend finishes their story. Then, tell them how I won the game.

1. Your parent is telling you what will happen that day. All of a sudden, you are thirsty.

   Volcano: _____

   Iceberg: _____

   _____

2. Your cousin comes over to play a game with you. You get bored and want to do something else.

   Volcano: _____

   Iceberg: _____

   _____

Name: _____ Date: _____

Find Ways to Help Others

An impulse does not have to be a bad thing. You may also have a strong desire to do something nice for someone. It is still a good idea to freeze and think.

Directions: Read each of the impulses. Write something nice you could do.

1. It's your dad's birthday. You have an impulse to do something special.

_____

_____

2. You hear your parent say that the living room is dirty. You have an impulse to do something kind.

_____

_____

3. You are missing your grandma. You have an impulse to do something nice.

_____

_____

4. Your sister got sick and is in bed. You have an impulse to check on her.

_____

_____

Focus on Family

Social Awareness

Name: _____ Date: _____

Focus on Family

Relationship Skills

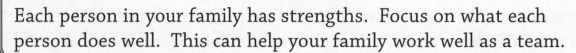

Teamwork

Each person in your family has strengths. Focus on what each person does well. This can help your family work well as a team.

Directions: Think about who in your family has each trait. Write how they show that trait.

1. Brave: _____

How do they show it?_____

_____

2. Smart: _____

How do they show it?_____

_____

3. Hard-working: _____

How do they show it?_____

_____

4. Honest: _____

How do they show it?_____

_____

Name: _____ **Date:** _____

Focus on Family

Responsible Decision-Making

Make Good Choices

Everyone makes mistakes. It is important to learn from them. That will help you make better choices in the future.

Directions: Read the stories. Write what each person should do.

Skip wakes up ready to play in the morning. His brother Ryan is grumpy until he eats.

1. When should Skip ask Ryan to play?_____

_____

Shae is reading. When she reads, she doesn't like people to make noises or talk to her. Her sister Mali has a question.

2. What should Mali do?_____

_____

Darius loves his cereal. His cousin Barry starts to make a snack. He notices there is only one bowl of Darius's cereal left.

3. What should Barry do?_____

_____

Name: _____ Date: _____

Worry

A feeling that something bad will happen is called *worry*. We all worry. Some things can worry you a little. Other things can worry you a lot.

Directions: Put each item on the scale next to how much you worry about it.

getting bad grades	losing your friends
getting hurt	making a mistake
getting into trouble	making new friends

Focus on Friends
Self-Awareness

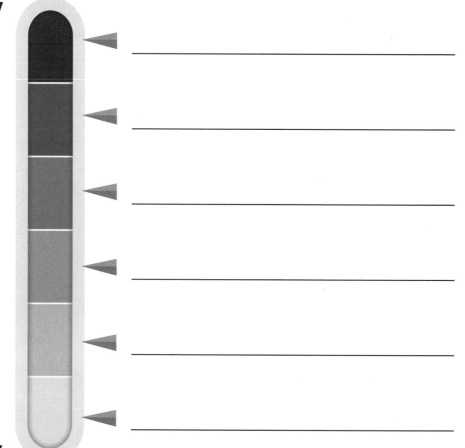

A Lot of Worry

_____

_____

_____

_____

_____

_____

Little Worry

Name: _____ Date: _____

Deal with Worry

We all worry. But how we deal with worry is a skill. You might deal with little worries one way and big worries another way.

Directions: Try each of these skills to help you deal with worry. Then, put them in order from least helpful to most helpful.

Soup Breathing

Hold your hands like you are holding a warm cup of soup. Smell the soup by taking a big sniff with your nose. Then, cool it off by blowing out of your mouth. Do this three times.

Stretch Out

Stand up and stretch your arms high over your head. Then, bend at your hips and touch your toes. Do this three times.

Move It

Do five jumping jacks, three push-ups, and five sit-ups. Do this three times.

1. _____

2. _____

3. _____

Name: _____ Date: _____

Notice When Others Are Worried

Your friends have worries, too. This may change the way they act. They may act nervous. They may get angry. You can be on the lookout for big feelings that are actually worry.

Focus on Friends
Social Awareness

Directions: Write how each person shows that they are worried.

1. James is starting at a new school.

_____

_____

2. Sylvia didn't practice for her piano lesson.

_____

_____

3. Charlie has a big game today.

_____

_____

4. Leesha's family was arguing last night.

_____

_____

Name: _____ Date: _____

Support Your Friends

You can help when you find out a friend is worried. This will help build better friendships.

Directions: Fill in the letter to show what you would do. Then, draw how you could help your worried friend.

1. Sully ripped his new pair of pants. He is worried about going home to tell his parents.

   Ⓐ Tell him that it was an accident.

   Ⓑ Help him practice talking to his parents.

2. Hannah left her lunch at home. She is worried that she won't be able to eat.

   Ⓐ Tell her that you will share your food.

   Ⓑ Go with her to ask a teacher for help.

Focus on Friends
Relationship Skills

Name: _____   Date: _____

Solve Problems

Sometimes, there are no adults around when a friend is worried. But that's okay. You can help friends by showing them how to relax.

Directions: Color the things that help you relax.

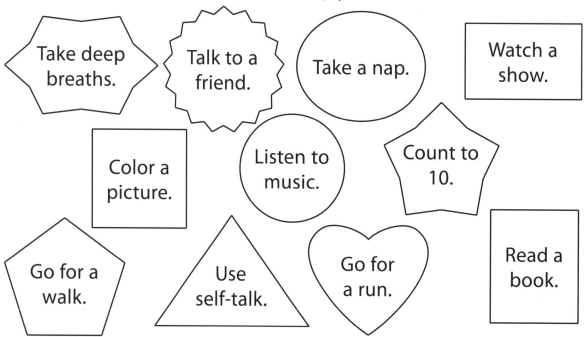

Take deep breaths.

Talk to a friend.

Take a nap.

Watch a show.

Color a picture.

Listen to music.

Count to 10.

Go for a walk.

Use self-talk.

Go for a run.

Read a book.

Directions: Create a flier to show friends what to do when they feel worried.

Name: _____ **Date:** _____

Be Honest

To be honest is to tell the truth. It can be hard to be honest. You might worry that you will get in trouble. But it feels better to be honest than to get away with a lie. You will also likely get into less trouble if you are honest.

Directions: Read each story. Fill in the letter of the honest choice.

1. Margaret is at the store. She is playing with a toy. She drops the toy and it breaks. What should she do?

   (A) Put the toy back on the shelf.

   (B) Tell an adult what happened.

2. Becki's family goes to a candy store for treats. She is so excited. She is jumping up and down. She bumps into a display and knocks candy on the floor. What should she do?

   (A) Tell an adult, and help clean up the mess.

   (B) Eat as much as she can so no one sees the spill.

3. Clark is riding his bike. He loses control and crashes into a parked car. He sees a scratch where his bike hit the car. What should he do?

   (A) Ride away as fast as he can.

   (B) Try to find the owners of the car to tell them what happened.

Name: _____ Date: _____

Focus on Community

Self-Management

Honesty and Kindness

Sometimes, the honest answer to a question is not kind. But you can still be honest. You just need to stop and think of a way to be both honest and kind.

Directions: Draw a line from the situation to the response that is both honest and kind.

You are trying on a shirt you don't like. Your mom loves it. She asks you what you think.	"He was okay. He showed off a little. But that's probably because he is really good."
You are at a community dinner. Your best friend's family brought green beans. They ask you if you liked their dish. You don't like green beans.	"They looked good. But green beans are not my favorite."
A friend shows you a drawing that they just did. They ask what you think. It looks pretty messy. You can't tell what it is.	"It looks like you worked hard on this drawing. Tell me how you did it."
A new kid comes to your soccer practice. He shows off a lot and steals the ball from you. Your parent asks you how you like the new kid.	"This shirt is really nice. It's just not my style. Can we find a different one?"

Name: _____ **Date:** _____

Notice Dishonesty

Sometimes, people do not tell the truth. This is called being *dishonest*. It is a skill to notice when other people are dishonest.

Directions: Write how you can tell that each person is being dishonest.

1.

_____

_____

2.

_____

_____

Name: _____ Date: _____

Focus on Community

Relationship Skills

Communicate Clearly

Sometimes, when people talk, they do not understand each other. This can lead to conflict. It can lead to hurt feelings. But you can learn to communicate clearly.

Directions: Read the Five Rules for CLEAR Communication.

Confident (Talk with a strong voice.)

Listen (Give the other person a chance to talk.)

Express your feelings (Say what you feel in a nice way.)

Attention (Pay attention.)

Repeat what you heard ("What I heard you say is....")

Directions: Read the story. Talk with a partner about how Lenny could use the five rules to talk to Abdul the next day.

Lenny and Abdul have plans to go to a movie. Ten minutes before they are supposed to leave, Abdul calls Lenny. He can't go. Lenny hears laughing in the background. He gets upset and hangs up the phone. Abdul did not get to explain that it was his brother laughing. Abdul really wanted to go.

© Shell Education

Name: _____ Date: _____

Forgiveness

All people make mistakes. People in your community will, too. You can decide to forgive. Or you can choose not to forgive. But that may ruin relationships.

Directions: Write what you think each person should do.

1. Donnie's coach yelled at him when he missed a ball. Donnie loves baseball. He did not like being yelled at.

   _____

   _____

2. August's friend, Simon, challenged him to a race. Simon won. He bragged about it. August felt embarrassed.

   _____

   _____

Directions: Write about a time when a friend made a mistake. If you forgave them, write about that. If you did not forgive them, write about what you could do now.

_____

_____

_____

_____

Name: _____ Date: _____

Focus on Self

Self-Awareness

Feelings Words

Knowing a lot of words for your feelings can help you. It can give an exact name to your own feelings.

Directions: Sort the words from most happy to least happy.

Most Happy

Happy Words

cheerful	merry
excited	peaceful
happy	sunny
joyful	thrilled

_____

_____

_____

_____

_____

_____

_____

_____

Least Happy

Directions: What other words mean happy? Fill the box with as many words as you can.

Name: _____ Date: _____

Manage Stress

There will be times when you do not feel happy. Stress can cause your body not to feel normal. Doing a body scan is a good way to manage stress. This is a way to check-in on your body.

Directions: Follow the steps to do a body scan. Then, rate how you feel.

Step 1: Find a quiet place to sit.

Step 2: Close your eyes.

Step 3: Spend five seconds thinking about each part of your body. How does each feel?

- head
- eyes
- mouth
- neck
- chest

- belly
- left arm/hand
- right arm/hand
- left leg/foot
- right leg/foot

Step 4: If any of these feels a little off, take three deep breaths as you think about it. Try to relax more with each breath.

Step 5: Open your eyes! You are done.

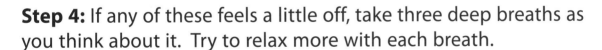

Directions: Circle the face that shows how you feel. To get the most out of a body scan, do it three times each day.

Name: _____   Date: _____

Focus on Self

Social Awareness

Show Concern for Other's Feelings

Your friends will feel sad sometimes. Making them laugh is a good start to helping them feel better. Trying to cheer someone up shows that you care about their feelings.

Directions: Work with a partner. Tell each other these jokes to see if you can make each other laugh.

1. **Joke:** What time do you need to go to the dentist?
   Answer: tooth-hurty (2:30)

2. **Joke:** What letter of the alphabet needs the most water?
   Answer: the *c* (sea)

3. **Joke:** Why did the student eat her homework?
   Answer: Her teacher said it was a piece of cake.

4. **Joke:** Why didn't the orange win the race?
   Answer: He ran out of juice.

5. **Joke:** Where do cows go on Friday nights?
   Answer: To the MOOvies.

Directions: Write your own favorite jokes.

1. _____

_____

2. _____

_____

Name: _____ **Date:** _____

Help Others Feel Better

It can take a lot of work to make a sad friend feel better. But it's a great way to be a good friend.

Directions: Read the ideas. Color three or more you could try the next time a friend is sad.

Say something nice about their clothes.

Say something you like about them (kind, helpful, friendly).

Invite them to spend time with you.

Write a hand-made card.

Make them a gift.

Talk about things you know they like.

Tell them a joke.

Clean something for them.

Offer to teach them something you know a lot about.

Invite them to play a game.

Ask to give them a hug.

Invite them to go on a walk.

Name: _____   Date: _____

Reflect about Your Friends

Who helps you feel better when you are sad? These people are the best kind of friends.

Directions: Answer the reflection questions.

1. When was the last time you were really sad?

   _____

2. What did you do to deal with your feelings?

   _____

   _____

3. Who helped you?

   _____

4. What did that person do?

   _____

   _____

Directions: Write a thank you note to that person.

Dear _____ ,

Thank you for _____

_____

Name: _____ **Date:** _____

Identity

Where you are from is part of your identity. The way you see yourself is, too. They help define who you are. Your identity can also include what you do in your neighborhood.

Directions: Design a T-shirt that shows off your identity. Here are some things you may want to include.

- where you are from
- things you like to do
- your neighbors
- your family

- your friends
- your favorite food
- your favorite place to go
- your own ideas!

Focus on Neighborhood

Self-Awareness

Name: _____   Date: _____

Focus on Neighborhood

Self-Management

Show Bravery

Do you know your neighbors? It takes bravery to meet new people. It also takes bravery to learn more about people you know. But knowing your neighbors well can help you feel safe.

Directions: Read these questions you could ask a neighbor. Write two of your own. Then, circle three you would like to try.

What is your name?

Where are you from?

What do you do for fun?

What kind of music do you like?

What is something you are proud of?

Who is someone special in your life?

What is your favorite TV show?

Who is your hero?

1. _____

2. _____

Challenge: Visit a neighbor with an adult. Ask them the questions you wrote and the ones you circled. If you don't live near anyone, talk to a teacher or other person at your school.

Name: _____ Date: _____

Work Together

Neighbors help each other. They work hard to keep each other safe. This builds a strong community.

Directions: Write how you could help each neighbor.

1. Darrel is riding his bike and falls off. His elbow is scratched, and his bike is broken.

   _____

   _____

2. Avery wants to play ball at the park. But she doesn't have a ball.

   _____

   _____

3. Parker is walking home from school. He drops his backpack, and all his papers fly out.

   _____

   _____

4. Riley sees someone break a window of a car. She tells you about it.

   _____

   _____

Focus on Neighborhood

Social Awareness

Name: _____ Date: _____

Teamwork

Teams can do more together than one person can do alone. Neighbors can work as teams, too. This is a good way to keep people safe.

Directions: Study the picture of the neighborhood. Circle the things you could fix as a team.

Directions: Choose one thing from the picture. Explain how you and a team would fix it.

_____

_____

_____

Name: _____ **Date:** _____

Neighborhood Choices

Some neighborhoods have their own rules. This helps neighbors work together to solve problems.

Directions: Each of these neighbors has a problem. Write what they should do.

1. Ian lives in an apartment. He noticed that the building doors do not close by themselves anymore. Cold weather is coming. He is worried that the building will get cold.

   _____

   _____

2. Mrs. Mason got injured. Now, it is hard for her to get to her mailbox down the street.

   _____

   _____

3. Howie lives on a quiet street. He has noticed a lot of trash in the street.

   _____

   _____

4. Suzie's neighbors play music very loudly. She has a hard time focusing on her homework.

   _____

   _____

Name: _____   Date: _____

Focus on School

Self-Awareness

Stand Up for Yourself

Standing up for yourself is a lot of work. You may need to stand up to your friends at school. You may even need to stand up to your teacher. Using clear communication is a good place to start.

Directions: Read each story. Write how each person can stand up for themselves. Use the Five Rules for CLEAR Communication.

> **C**onfident (Talk with a strong voice.)
>
> **L**isten (Give the other person a chance to talk.)
>
> **E**xpress your feelings (Say what you feel in a nice way.)
>
> **A**ttention (Pay attention.)
>
> **R**epeat what you heard ("What I heard you say is....")

1. Hoda is at recess. She is playing with a jump rope. Kyle tells the teacher that she was using it to hit other kids. She was not.

   _____

   _____

   _____

2. Lawrence is in art class. The teacher tells the students to cut the paper. But he doesn't have any scissors.

   _____

   _____

   _____

Name: _____ Date: _____

Set Goals

The more you practice something, the better you get at it. If you want to be a better reader, read more. If you want to be a better artist, do more art. Setting a practice goal will keep you on track.

Directions: Choose one thing from the list you would like to do better. Or think of your own.

reading more at one time	remembering math facts
reading more smoothly	finishing work on time
making friends	running faster
staying calm	being more helpful

Directions: Answer the questions to make a plan.

1. What did you choose?

_____

2. How will you practice?

_____

_____

3. How much time will you practice each day?

_____

Focus on School

Self-Management

Name: _____ Date:_____

Empathy

Empathy is being able to understand what someone else is feeling. You don't need to have ever felt the same way. You just need to try to understand. Empathy is a skill you can learn. But it takes a lot of practice.

Focus on School

Social Awareness

Directions: Imagine you are a character from a book, movie, or TV show. Write a letter to a friend as that character. Describe a problem you had. Explain how you solved it. Share any lessons you learned.

Character: _____

Dear _____ ,

_____

_____

_____

_____

_____

_____

_____

Sincerely, _____

Apologies

You may make a friend feel sad someday. You should apologize if you do. An apology is when you say you are sorry. Doing this in an honest way can help your friend feel less sad. You can't take back what you did. But an apology can make your friend feel better.

Directions: Read about what makes a good apology. Then, write an apology for each picture.

A good apology has a few important parts.

- Make eye contact.
- Speak clearly.
- Explain what you are sorry for.
- Offer a way to make things better.

1. _____

   _____

   _____

2. _____

   _____

   _____

Focus on School
Relationship Skills

Name: _____ Date: _____

Focus on School

Responsible Decision-Making

Make Safe Choices

If you stop and think to make good choices, you can stay safe at school.

Directions: List things that are safe to do at school. List things that are not safe to do at school.

Safe	Not Safe

Directions: Draw yourself being safe at school.

Know Your Role Model

There are people in your community you can look up to. Those people are role models. They set good examples. They are also people who help you.

Directions: Write a letter to someone you look up to. Tell them why they are your role model.

Dear _____ ,

_____

_____

_____

_____

Sincerely, _____

Directions: Draw yourself with your role model.

Focus on Community

Self-Awareness

Name: _____ **Date:** _____

Manage Stress

Many second graders are in a lot of activities. Those activities can be fun! But they can also make you busy. It can be hard to go to school all day, and then go to an activity. It can all make you feel stressed. Knowing how to manage stress can help.

Directions: Follow the steps to manage stress.

Deflate the Balloon

Step 1: Imagine that your lungs are big balloons.

Step 2: Suck in as much air as you can to make your lungs as full as they can be.

Step 3: Hold onto the air for five seconds.

Step 4: Just like a balloon, let the air blow out of you.

Directions: Inside the balloon, draw a place where you feel stressed.

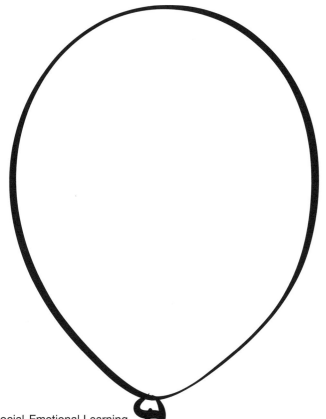

Name: _____ Date: _____

Benefits of Your Community

Communities have a lot of benefits. Benefits are things that make life better. One benefit is that they give us ways to have fun!

Directions: Pretend a new kid moved in next door. Draw the benefits in your community that you would tell them about.

Name: _____ Date: _____

Make Good Friends

No one is perfect. It's always good to hear. Your friends will do things that are not perfect. You have to remind yourself of the good things about them.

Directions: Choose three friends in your community. List things you like about them.

Name: _____

Things you like about them: _____

_____

Name: _____

Things you like about them: _____

_____

Name: _____

Things you like about them: _____

_____

Name: _____ **Date:** _____

Small and Big Problems

It is normal to get stuck when trying to solve a problem. Sometimes, you have a small problem. Those you can solve on your own. But sometimes, you have big problems. You will need help from an adult to solve those.

Directions: List big and small problems in your community.

Small Problems	Big Problems

Directions: Choose one of the small problems from your list. Draw how you would solve it.

Name: _____   Date: _____

Use a Mantra

A mantra is a short phrase that you repeat to yourself. It can help calm your mind. It can help you face hard things. A mantra also reminds you of the good things in your life.

Directions: Read these mantras. Color three that would help you most.

I love and approve of myself.

I trust myself.

Wonderful things will happen to me.

I forgive myself for my mistakes.

I let go of my anger.

I will show my friends that I care about them.

I will choose friends who love me.

I will work hard and try my best.

I am loved.

I am amazing!

Name: _____ Date: _____

Accepting a Loss

No one likes to lose. It can make you feel angry. It takes practice to learn to accept a loss. But learning how will help you feel less angry.

Directions: Read the different ways to accept a loss.

Shake hands and say, "Good game."	Offer a high five.	Say to yourself, *I still had fun.*
Ask if the person wants to play again.	Say to yourself, *It's only a game.*	Say to yourself, *Next time will be different.*
Start practicing for next time.	Say, "Good job!" to the person or team who won.	Think about how hard you worked to get this far.

Directions: Write what each person could do or say to accept their loss. Use the examples above. Or create your own.

1. Chuck didn't get the part he wanted in a play.

   _____

   _____

2. Hakeem did not win his piano competition.

   _____

   _____

3. Brayden's football team lost the state championship.

   _____

   _____

Name: _____ Date: _____

Point of View

There is often more than one way to see the same thing. You can help solve conflicts by thinking about others' points of view. You can try to see the world the way other people do.

Directions: Read the story. Try to see both points of view. Then, answer the questions.

Kendall and Holly are good friends. Kendall's mom told her she could invite three friends for her birthday. She wanted to invite Holly. But there was not enough room. Holly heard Kendall inviting other people. She thought they were friends. Holly does not think it is fair.

1. How does Kendall feel?

_____

2. How does Holly feel?

_____

3. What is the problem from Kendall's point of view?

_____

4. What is the problem from Holly's point of view?

_____

5. How could Kendall and Holly solve this conflict?

_____

_____

Name: _____ **Date:** _____

Listening Skills

Good listening skills will help you be a better friend. You should try to listen twice as much as you talk.

Directions: Follow the steps. Then, answer the questions.

- Look at the person talking to you. Color the eyes.
- Keep your hands quiet. Color the hands.
- Turn on your brain to think about what is being said. Color the head.
- Keep your body still. Color the arms and legs.
- Ask a question. This is the best way to show you're listening. Color the rest of the picture.

Focus on Self

Relationship Skills

1. How could listening help you learn more?

   _____

   _____

2. How could listening help you be a better friend?

   _____

   _____

Name: _____   Date: _____

Critical Thinking

Critical thinking means to think on your own to solve a problem. Some problems are tough. But they can seem easier if you look at them from another point of view. You might think, *What would my role model do?*

Directions: The people we look up to are role models. Read the problems. Write how your role model would solve them.

1. You are supposed to take out the trash before you play outside with your friends. But your friend is at the door and wants to play right now.

   _____

   _____

2. You are working on a tough math problem. Nothing seems to make sense. You want to give up.

   _____

   _____

3. You have a chance to make the winning shot at the end of the game. But you miss, and your team loses.

   _____

   _____

4. You are at a store. You see someone stealing clothes.

   _____

   _____

Name: _____ Date: _____

Your Impact

Your actions can have an impact on others. If you are kind, then others may be kind, too. If you are mean, others may choose to be mean.

Directions: Read the situations. Answer the questions.

1. Leroy is at a football game with his friends. He yells, "Hey, losers! We are going to wipe the floor with you." How might Leroy's words affect his friends?

   _____

   _____

2. Mateo and a friend are at the neighborhood pool. A group of boys starts to tease his friend. Mateo tells them to knock it off. How might Mateo's actions affect his friend?

   _____

   _____

3. Mackenzie is at the mall with her friends. Her mom tells her it's time to go home. She wants to seem cool in front of her friends. She calls her mom lame and rolls her eyes. How might Mackenzie's actions affect her mom?

   _____

   _____

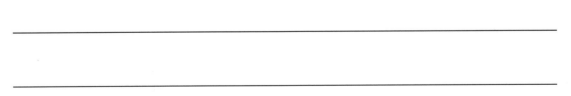

Name: _____ Date: _____

Focus on Neighborhood

Self-Management

Choose Kindness

If you have a hard time solving a conflict, choose kindness. Sometimes, this means you will need to freeze and calm down. Big problems can cause big feelings. When you have big feelings, you can do things you regret.

Directions: Read each conflict. Fill in the letter to show the kind way to solve it.

1. Lee sees a person in a wheelchair trying to get into the library. The door is not working.

   Ⓐ Lee should hold open the door.

   Ⓑ Lee should ignore them and walk past.

2. Mohammad is with his sister at a park. A group of kids start to make fun of his sister.

   Ⓐ Mohammad should tell them to stop in a calm and strong voice.

   Ⓑ Mohammad should run over and hit them.

3. Monica is practicing for her basketball game. Two kids come onto the court and tell her to leave.

   Ⓐ Monica should yell at the kids and tell them she has every right to be there.

   Ⓑ Monica should explain that she has a big game. She can tell them she'll be done soon and ask them to join her.

4. Evan is wearing a new shirt that he loves. His best friend says it's not really his style.

   Ⓐ Evan should tell his friend he has bad taste, and his clothes look ugly.

   Ⓑ Evan should use self-talk and think, *I know it looks cool*.

Name: _____ Date: _____

Different Rules

Every place needs to have its own set of rules. This is because they need to keep people safe.

Directions: Write a different rule each place would have.

_____

_____

_____

_____

_____

_____

_____

_____

_____

_____

_____

_____

Name: _____ Date: _____

Focus on Neighborhood

Relationship Skills

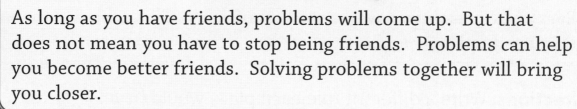

Problem Solving

As long as you have friends, problems will come up. But that does not mean you have to stop being friends. Problems can help you become better friends. Solving problems together will bring you closer.

Directions: Read the story. Answer the questions.

Margo and Anita are on the same softball team. Anita has played first base for a long time. The coach moves Margo to first base. Margo is really good. Anita does not know if she will ever get to play first base again.

1. How does Margo feel?

_____

2. How does Anita feel?

_____

3. What problem do they have?

_____

_____

4. How can they work together to solve this problem?

_____

_____

_____

Name: _____ **Date:** _____

Impact of Your Decisions

When you throw a rock into water, it makes ripples. The ripples spread over the water. The ripples last long after the rock is gone. Your decisions are like the rock. The things you do impact a lot of other people. They can have an impact for a long time.

Directions: Read each decision. Think about how each one could affect other people.

Kami wanders into her neighbor's yard. She takes a brand new football and runs out of the yard. When she gets home, her parents ask her about the ball. She says she found it at the park.

1. How does Kami's decision affect her neighbor?

_____

2. How does Kami's decision affect her parents?

_____

Leon is riding his bike in his neighborhood. He gets a little too close to a car and scratches it. Leon rushes home. His parents ask him what happened to his bike. He says he fell off, but he does not tell them about the car.

3. How does Leon's decision affect his neighbor?

_____

4. How does Leon's decision affect his parents?

_____

Name: _____ Date: _____

Focus on School

Self-Awareness

The Power of *Yet*

Using the word *yet* can help change your brain. It can be sad to think about things you do not know how to do. But if you just add the word *yet*, you can see things differently. *Yet* is a powerful word!

Directions: Add the word *yet* to the end of each sentence. Notice how different each one feels.

1. I do not know how to skip _____.

2. I do not read very well _____.

3. I do not do math very quickly _____.

Directions: Write things you know how to do on the outside of the word. Write things you do not know how to do YET on the inside.

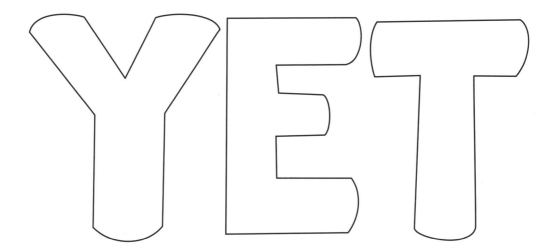

Name: _____ Date: _____

Use *Yet* to Set Goals

Using the word *yet* can help you set goals. Learning new things can be hard work. It can seem to take forever. But it helps to remember that you are learning a little more every day. Set small goals to help you slowly get better. Lots of small goals add up to big progress.

Directions: Read the story. Then, write and draw your own.

Julia thought math was hard. She set a goal to learn more math facts. She said, "I do not know all my math facts yet." She started to use flash cards. She studied just a few each day. The next day, she practiced a few more. After a few weeks, she had memorized all her math facts.

1. Write your own story about one of your goals.

_____

_____

_____

_____

2. Draw a picture to go with your story.

Self-Management

Focus on School

Name: _____ Date: _____

Focus on School

Social Awareness

Use *Yet* to See Others' Strengths

Using the word *yet* can help you see what you can do. It can also help you see what your friends can do.

Directions: Write sentences using the word *yet* to help each of these friends.

1. Kim gets really sad at reading time. Her reading sounds very choppy. She wants to read more smoothly.

   _____

   _____

2. Chip gets frustrated in P.E. He can't run as fast as everyone else.

   _____

   _____

3. Cameron does not like music class. He wants to sing better. But he never seems to hit the right notes.

   _____

   _____

4. Ava can't tie her shoes. She gets angry when she has an untied shoe.

   _____

   _____

Name: _____ **Date:** _____

Use *Yet* to Work Together

You do not have to use the power of *yet* alone. You can use it when you work with others. In fact, working as a team makes *yet* even more powerful.

Directions: Read the six benefits of working on a team.

Find more creative thinking.

Take healthier risks.

Use each other's strengths.

Build trust.

Find pride in finishing something.

Build stronger friendships.

Directions: Draw a picture of a time when you and others worked as a team. Then, answer the question.

1. How does your picture show the power of *yet*?

_____

_____

_____

Name: _____ Date: _____

Celebrate Your Success!

It is important to celebrate your success. You deserve it! It will also help you keep going.

Directions: Answer the questions to plan a party to celebrate your success. Use the ideas in the table, or use your own ideas.

Guests	Activities
friends	dancing
parents	cooking or baking
grandparents	playing games
brothers or sisters	watching a movie
neighbors	doing arts and crafts
pets	playing a sport

1. What success will you celebrate?

_____

2. Who will you invite?

_____

_____

3. What will you do?

_____

_____

Name: _____ Date: _____

Your Gift to the Community

You are a gift! You have worked so hard this year. You have learned skills. You have practiced ways to be a better friend. You will be able to use these new skills in your community.

Directions: Circle your best skills. Draw yourself using one of those skills in your community. Then, answer the questions.

communication	working on a team
thinking about others	setting goals
being brave	making good friends
problem-solving	being honest
staying organized	controlling your emotions

1. What skill do you want to improve?

_____

2. Who could help you practice this skill?

_____

Name: _____ Date: _____

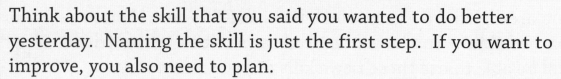

Get Help Setting Goals

Think about the skill that you said you wanted to do better yesterday. Naming the skill is just the first step. If you want to improve, you also need to plan.

Focus on Community

Self-Management

Directions: Answer the questions to make a plan.

1. Which skill did you choose to improve? Why?

_____

2. How will this skill help you?

_____

3. What will you need to practice?

_____

4. When can you work on this skill?

_____

5. How long will it take to get better?

_____

6. Draw a picture showing you after you have learned the skill.

 126958—180 Days of Social-Emotional Learning

Being Grateful

It is important to be grateful. This is true when someone helps you grow. It is true when someone teaches you a new skill. Be creative in how you say thank you.

Directions: Design an award for someone who has helped you grow. Include each of the things in the box.

- a creative design
- the person's name
- how they helped you
- your name

Focus on Community
Social Awareness

Name: _____ Date: _____

Be a Leader

You have so many new skills! You can be a leader in your community. One way to be a leader is to set a good example.

Directions: Read each situation. Write how you could set a good example.

1. Two people on your soccer team are fighting. They both want to play goalie.

   _____

   _____

2. Your sister wants to make the softball team. Tryouts are a week away.

   _____

   _____

3. You see a group of people at a playground. They are being very unsafe.

   _____

   _____

4. Your best friend does not know how to ride a skateboard. You are very good.

   _____

   _____

Focus on Community

Relationship Skills

Name: _____ **Date:** _____

Keep Growing

You can keep growing. You can keep improving. Keep pushing yourself. Keep learning new skills. You can do anything! Small good decisions can add up to huge gains.

Directions: Write things you are proud of on each coin. Then, color the bucket.

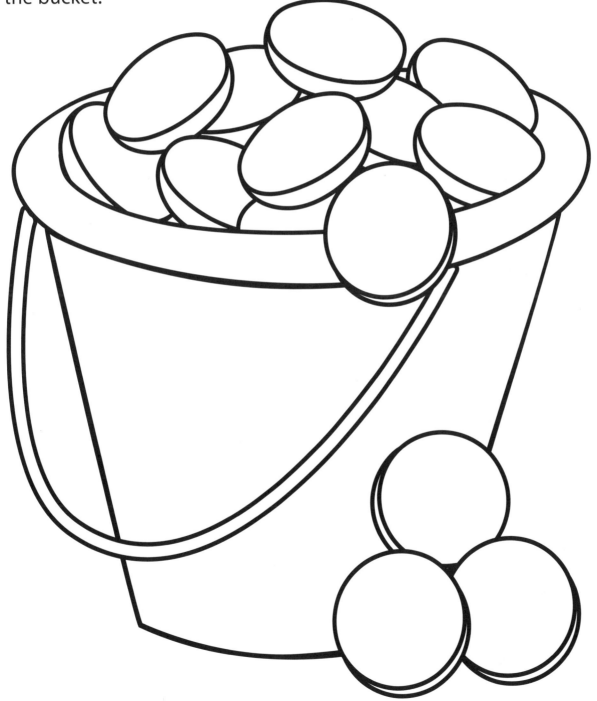

Answer Key

There are many open-ended drawing and writing prompts in this book. Many answers will vary. Examples are given when needed.

Week 1 Day 3 (page 14)
1. Jessica is feeling sad.
2. Mark is feeling happy.

Week 1 Day 4 (page 15)
All items except *Tell someone they can't play with you* and *Take someone's pencil that they left on the table* should be colored.

Week 3 Day 3 (page 24)
1. He loves baseball.
2. He jumps up and down.
3. She does not like this project.
4. She puts her hands on her head, takes a deep breath, puts her head down, and pushes her paper away.

Week 3 Day 5 (page 26)
1. B
2. A
3. A
4. B

Week 4 Day 4 (page 30)
Circle: Children playing on a playground together; two children laughing together

X: "Boys Only" sign; the child with all the toys

Week 4 Day 5 (page 31)
Problems: lit match; playing in the street; not wearing a seatbelt

Solutions: Examples: blow out the match; play in the front or backyard; put seatbelt on

Week 5 Day 1 (page 32)
Examples:
1. clenched teeth, fist, and jaw; body stiff and a heated face
2. smiling
3. crying, frown face, puffed out lip
4. face looks worried, trembling, touching face

Week 5 Day 4 (page 35)
eyes: crying

mouth: open

hand: rubbing face

Week 6 Day 1 (page 37)
***Xs* through:** A boy tells a girl that she can't play football; A girl takes a doll away from a boy.

Week 6 Day 5 (page 41)
Examples:
1. The ball could hit the car and break a window, or the children could get hit by the car.
2. The child could get hurt because she isn't wearing a helmet.
3. The water could ruin the computer.

Week 7 Day 5 (page 46)
Big problems: You see smoke coming from a tablet; Mayra falls and breaks her foot; Javier takes food from your lunch.

Small problems: Kelly takes your pencil; Aimee is thirsty; Perry can't find his boot.

Bekkah and Dante could play Rock, Paper, Scissors to see who goes first; They could take turns going first; One of them could let the other one just go.

Week 8 Day 2 (page 48)
1. There was a lot of trash on the sidewalk.
2. Layla told her dad.
3. They picked up trash.

Week 8 Day 3 (page 49)
Examples:

Swimming Pool: Walk by the water, no splashing, no diving in the shallow end.

Public Library: No running, check out books, don't climb on the shelves.

School: Listen to your teacher, stay with your class, use kind words.

Home: Don't play with fire, follow directions, don't turn the water too hot.

Week 9 Day 1 (page 52)
Use for Self-Talk: I am going to keep trying; I believe in myself; I can do hard things; I can learn how to do this; I will try a different way; Learning is fun.

Don't Use for Self-Talk: I am going to fail; I am not that smart; I can't do this; This is too hard.

Answer Key *(cont.)*

Week 9 Day 3 (page 54)

You can't find a book to read—librarian

You need help finding a clean pair of socks—sibling or cousin

You are looking for someone to play with—best friend

You broke a window at your house—parent or caretaker

You ran out of paper at school—teacher

Week 9 Day 4 (page 55)

1. He kicks the ball on the inside of his foot.
2. He has more control of the ball.
3. He runs faster.

Week 10 Day 2 (page 58)

Examples:

1. wash the dishes
2. tidy up the living room
3. take out the trash

Week 11 Day 1 (page 62)

Examples:

1. Let's play something else instead.
2. Please stop. That's not nice.
3. No, I'm not comfortable doing that.
4. I don't want to do that. Let's do something else.

Week 11 Day 3 (page 64)

Circle: picking up trash; sharing a pencil

Week 11 Day 4 (page 65)

1. Jamar draws the fox.
2. Tonya helps Jamar read a book that is too hard for him to read.
3. They both felt proud of their hard work.

Week 11 Day 5 (page 66)

1. react
2. respond
3. react
4. respond
5. respond
6. react

Week 12 Day 3 (page 69)

1. The two students did the same thing, but Luis got into more trouble.
2. Example: The teacher should ask both students to stop talking.
3. Jin and Rasheed were both yelling, but only Jin had to leave.
4. Example: Both children should have to go home for the day.

Week 12 Day 5 (page 71)

1. Cut the grass.
2. Wash off the car.
3. Clean up the yard.
4. Offer to help carry some boxes.

Week 13 Day 3 (page 74)

1. Erin is feeling scared because she can't swim very well.
2. Example: Jemma could offer to move to the shallow end.
3. Milo is feeling embarrassed about scoring a goal for the other team.
4. Example: Roman could say that we all make mistakes and this is only a game.

Week 13 Day 4 (page 75)

1. Lose-Lose
2. Win-Win
3. Win-Lose

Week 14 Day 1 (page 77)

Mad: angry, furious, upset
Happy: cheerful, excited, silly
Sad: blue, gloomy, unhappy
Shy: fearful, nervous, scared

Week 14 Day 2 (page 78)

1. The child is taking some time to be alone.
2. The child is closing his eyes and taking some time alone.

Week 14 Day 3 (page 79)

You keep the money: I would feel bad; The person would be upset.

You turn the money in at the office: I would feel proud; The person would be grateful.

Answer Key *(cont.)*

Week 15 Day 2 (page 83)

Examples:

1. Study 10 minutes every day.
2. Make up a rhyme to remember what each sign means.
3. Practice writing every day.
4. Watch videos online about how to skateboard. Then, try some basic steps.

Week 15 Day 5 (page 86)

Examples:

1. Only click on learning apps when doing schoolwork.
2. Take a deep breath after losing a game.
3. Think about others' feelings before speaking.
4. Use self-talk to remind herself she'll get a turn.

Week 16 Day 2 (page 88)

You spill juice on your favorite shirt—I love this shirt. I can try to get the stain out when I get home.

You are at a fair, and your favorite ride is broken—I am so bummed. But there are other rides I enjoy.

You are going to a movie at the theater. When you get there, the movie is sold out—I really wanted to see that movie. I know I can see it another time.

You are excited to try the cookies your big sister made. They are all gone before you get one—I really wanted to try one. I'll ask my sister if she can make some more.

Week 16 Day 3 (page 89)

Examples:

1. Juan still gets to go swimming.
2. Darla has some money to buy something.
3. Jessica is on a team and got to play.
4. Roman gets to play at a park, and other things might be open.

Week 16 Day 5 (page 91)

1. King spoke about unfair laws.
2. King stood up for himself and others.
3. Anthony fought for women's right to vote.
4. Anthony spoke up when things were unfair.

Week 17 Day 1 (page 92)

1. medium
2. big
3. small
4. medium
5. big
6. medium

Week 17 Day 2 (page 93)

Examples:

1. Find another eraser, or cross something out.
2. Ask them to be more careful.
3. Use self-talk to remind yourself that it will be okay, and that no one probably noticed.
4. Play on the swings instead.
5. Find something fun to do at your house.
6. Remove the bruised part, or eat around it.

Week 17 Day 4 (page 95)

Color: Close your eyes; use positive self-talk; stop and think; ask for a break; get an adult; ask for help; think of another way; talk about your choices; count down from 10; take a deep breath; stay calm; say, "I can do this!"

X: Hide in your room; call someone a name; push someone; steal something; make a mean face; throw something; yell; give up.

Week 17 Day 5 (page 96)

Throw the bowl of cereal: No
Take a deep breath: Yes
Throw the remote: No

Week 18 Day 1 (page 97)

1. sad; unhappy
2. shy; scared
3. happy; excited
4. mad; angry

Week 19 Day 2 (page 103)

I feel annoyed when Izzy doesn't share.

Answer Key *(cont.)*

Week 19 Day 3 (page 104)

1. Erin is feeling hurt and mad that she got hit by a bike.
2. Kyle is feeling embarrassed about running into Erin with his bike.
3. Luke is frustrated that he lost.
4. Rocky is mad that his friend is calling him a cheater.

Week 19 Day 4 (page 105)

1. Justin yelled the message. He should have used a calm and confident voice.
   New I-Message: I feel mad when people take my food. Next time, will you please leave my food alone?
2. Vivi whispered and was not confident. She should have talked more clearly.
   New I-Message: I feel annoyed when people trip me. Next time, will you please slow down?

Week 19 Day 5 (page 106)

1. no
2. yes
3. yes
4. no

Week 20 Day 2 (page 108)

1. a gardener
2. a swim coach
3. a nurse or someone in nursing school
4. an artist or an art teacher

Week 20 Day 4 (page 110)

Circle: able to set goals; positive; helpful; cares about others; good listener; reliable; creative; trustworthy

Week 21 Day 2 (page 113)

Circle: You drop your device. The screen cracks; You forgot your password; Your app crashes. You can't get it to open again.

Week 21 Day 3 (page 114)

Someone beats you in a game—"Nice game. Let's play again."

Your friend hurts your feelings—"What you said really hurt my feelings."

Someone you do not know tries to message you—Delete and ignore messages from strangers.

Week 21 Day 4 (page 115)

1. The words are the same; one is calm, and one is yelling.
2. Most of the words are the same; one says *want*, and the other *will not*.
3. Most of the words are the same; one uses full words, and the other uses an abbreviation.

Week 21 Day 5 (page 116)

Examples:

1. You could get into trouble for not getting off your device on time. You may not get as much screen time next time.
2. You could get into trouble and not be able to use the devices anymore.
3. You might have to clean up all the wasted paper.
4. The keyboard could be ruined.

Week 22 Day 4 (page 120)

A group of friends sees a person at the park with a dirty shirt. They start to tease him: "That is not cool! You shouldn't make fun of people. He might be having a bad day."

A teammate on your basketball team slips and the ball goes out of bounds. Your team laughs at him. "Hey, it's not nice to laugh at people. It was just a mistake. It could happen to any of us."

A friend tells a group of neighbors that he has to go home for dinner. They start to tease him. They call him a baby: "Come on, he is just eating with his family. Lay off of him."

A group of neighbors is going to play a video game together. One person says she is not allowed to play that game. The group starts to tease her: "It's no big deal! She is just trying to do what her parents told her. Let's go do something we all can do."

Week 22 Day 5 (page 121)

1. A
2. B

Week 23 Day 1 (page 122)

From top to bottom: rage, fuming, outraged, mad, upset, frustrated, annoyed, irritated

Answer Key (cont.)

Week 23 Day 5 (page 126)
1. small
2. big
3. big
4. small
5. small
6. small
7. big
8. big

Week 24 Day 3 (page 129)
1. Claire was mad that she struck out. She could be embarrassed.
2. Keisha was upset that someone cut her in line. She may not like when things are not fair.
3. Ronald was angry that his boots got dirty. They may be very special.
4. Keefer was fuming because someone was stealing books. He doesn't like when people are not honest.

Week 25 Day 5 (page 136)
1. A
2. B
3. C

Week 26 Day 1 (page 137)
1. The child is not going to get the candy bar. "It's ok, maybe I'll get one next time."
2. The child wants to play on the device. "If I stay calm, I will get to use my tablet again."
3. The child is disappointed about how they did on the test. "I know I can do better next time."

Week 26 Day 5 (page 141)
1. Skip should wait until his brother has eaten breakfast.
2. Mali should wait until Shae is done reading.
3. Barry should make a different snack.

Week 27 Day 3 (page 144)
1. He is hiding behind his mom.
2. She is biting her nails.
3. His stomach hurts.
4. She is looking down and not talking to anyone.

Week 28 Day 1 (page 147)
1. B
2. A
3. B

Week 28 Day 2 (page 148)

You are trying on a shirt you don't like. Your mom loves it. She asks you what you think—"This shirt is really nice. It's just not my style. Can we find a different one?"

You are at a community dinner. Your best friend's family brought green beans. They ask you if you liked their dish. You don't like green beans—"They looked good. But green beans are not my favorite."

A friend shows you a drawing that they just did. They ask what you think. It looks pretty messy. You can't tell what it is—"It looks like you worked hard on this drawing. Tell me how you did it."

A new kid comes to your soccer practice. He shows off a lot and steals the ball from you. Your parent asks you how you like the new kid—"He was ok. He showed off a little. But that's probably because he is really good."

Week 29 Day 1 (page 152)

From top to bottom: thrilled, excited, joyful, merry, sunny, cheerful, happy, peaceful

Week 30 Day 3 (page 159)

Examples:
1. Help him off the street, and get him bandages.
2. Let her borrow my ball.
3. Help him pick up the papers.
4. Tell an adult what happened.

Week 30 Day 4 (page 160)

Examples: pick up trash, water plants, clean up walls

Week 30 Day 5 (page 161)

Examples:
1. Ask an adult to report the problem to the building manager.
2. Ask a neighbor to get her mail for her.
3. Pick up trash with some friends.
4. Ask an adult to talk to her neighbors about their loud music.

Answer Key *(cont.)*

Week 31 Day 4 (page 165)

Examples:

1. I'm sorry I broke your pencil. Let me sharpen it for you.
2. I'm sorry I tripped you. Can I get you some ice?

Week 33 Day 3 (page 174)

1. Kendall feels bad about not being able to invite Holly over for her party.
2. Holly feels hurt because she wasn't invited to the party.
3. Kendall is stuck because her mom told her she could only invite three friends.
4. Holly thinks that Kendall is her friend, but she is leaving her out of the party.
5. Kendall and Holly could find a different day to meet together and do something fun.

Week 34 Day 1 (page 177)

1. Leroy's friends might start to say mean things, too.
2. Mateo's friend might be grateful and share that kindness with others.
3. Mackenzie's mom might have hurt feelings, and Mackenzie might get in trouble.

Week 34 Day 2 (page 178)

1. A
2. A
3. B
4. B

Week 34 Day 3 (page 179)

Examples:

Park: Don't climb up the slide; take turns on the equipment; don't push people; be kind to others.

Library: Be respectful of others; don't write on the books; don't climb on the shelves; don't yell.

School: Listen to your teacher; follow along with your class; don't climb on tables; walk in the hallways.

House: Ask before getting a snack; listen to adults; be respectful; be kind to your siblings.

Week 34 Day 4 (page 180)

1. Margo feels proud that she is doing so well at first base.
2. Anita feels worried that she may never play first base again.
3. They both are good at first base, but only one can play.
4. Margo can practice with Anita, or they could talk to the coach.

Week 34 Day 5 (page 181)

1. Kami's neighbor will be upset.
2. Kami might lose her parents' trust.
3. Leon's neighbor will have to pay to get the car fixed.
4. Leon's parents will be upset.

Week 35 Day 3 (page 184)

1. Kim can't read smoothly yet.
2. Chip can't run as fast as everyone else yet.
3. Cameron can't sing well yet.
4. Ava can't tie her shoes yet.

References Cited

The Aspen Institute: National Commission on Social, Emotional, & Academic Development. 2018. "From a Nation at Risk to a Nation at Hope." https://nationathope.org/wp-content/uploads/2018_aspen_final-report_full_webversion.pdf.

Collaborative for Academic, Social, and Emotional Learning (CASEL). n.d. "What Is SEL?" Last modified December 2020. https://casel.org/what-is-sel/.

Durlak, Joseph A., Roger P. Weissberg, Allison B. Dymnicki, Rebecca D. Taylor, and Kriston B. Schellinger. 2011. "The Impact of Enhancing Students' Social and Emotional Learning: A Meta-Analysis of School-Based Universal Interventions." *Child Development* 82 (1): 405–32.

Goleman, Daniel. 2005. *Emotional Intelligence: Why It Can Matter More Than IQ.* New York: Bantam Dell.

Palmer, Parker J. 2007. *The Courage to Teach: Exploring the Inner Landscape of a Teacher's Life.* San Francisco: Jossey-Bass.

Name: _____ Date: _____

Connecting to Self Rubric

Days 1 and 2

Directions: Complete this rubric every six weeks to evaluate students' Day 1 and Day 2 activity sheets. Only one rubric is needed per student. Their work over the six weeks can be considered together. Appraise their work in each category by circling or highlighting the descriptor in each row that best describes the student's work. Then, consider the student's overall progress in connecting to self. In the box, draw ☆, ✓+ , or ✓ to indicate your overall evaluation.

Competency	Advanced	Satisfactory	Developing
Self-Awareness	Can accurately identify one's own full range of emotions.	Identifies one's own emotions accurately most of the time.	Has trouble identifying their own feelings.
	Understands that thoughts and feelings are connected.	Sees the connection of thoughts and feelings most of the time.	Does not connect thoughts to feelings.
	Can identify strengths and areas of growth.	Can identify a few strengths and weaknesses.	Can identify only one strength or weakness.
Self-Management	Can manage stress by using several different strategies.	Manages stress with only one strategy.	Does not manage stress well.
	Shows motivation in all areas of learning.	Shows motivation in a few areas of learning.	Shows little to no motivation.
	Is able to set realistic goals.	Sets some goals that are realistic and some that are not.	Has a hard time setting goals that are achievable.

Comments

_____

_____

_____

_____

Overall

☐

Name: _____ Date: _____

Relating to Others Rubric

Days 3 and 4

Directions: Complete this rubric every six weeks to evaluate students' Day 3 and Day 4 activity sheets. Only one rubric is needed per student. Their work over the six weeks can be considered together. Appraise their work in each category by circling or highlighting the descriptor in each row that best describes the student's work. Then, consider the student's overall progress in relating to others. In the box, draw ☆, ✓+, or ✓ to indicate your overall evaluation.

Competency	Advanced	Satisfactory	Developing
Social Awareness	Shows empathy toward others.	Shows empathy toward others most of the time.	Shows little to no empathy toward others.
	Can explain how rules are different in different places.	Knows that some places can have different rules.	Is not able to articulate how rules may change in different places.
	Can list many people who support them in their learning.	Can list some people who support them in their learning.	Can list few people who support them in their learning.
Relationship Skills	Uses a variety of strategies to solve conflicts with peers.	Has a few strategies to solve conflicts with peers.	Struggles to solve conflicts with peers.
	Uses advanced skills of listening and paraphrasing while communicating.	Is able to communicate effectively.	Has breakdowns in communication skills.
	Works effectively with a team. Shows leadership in accomplishing team goals.	Works effectively with a team most of the time.	Has trouble working with others on a team.

Comments

_____

_____

_____

_____

Overall

© Shell Education

Name: _____ Date: _____

Making Decisions Rubric

Day 5

Directions: Complete this rubric every six weeks to evaluate students' Day 5 activity sheets. Only one rubric is needed per student. Their work over the six weeks can be considered together. Appraise their work in each category by circling or highlighting the descriptor in each row that best describes the student's work. Then, consider the student's overall progress in making decisions. In the box, draw ☆, ✓+, or ✓ to indicate your overall evaluation.

Competency	Advanced	Satisfactory	Developing
Responsible Decision-Making	Makes decisions that benefit their own long-term interests.	Makes decisions that are sometimes impulsive and sometimes thought out.	Is impulsive and has a hard time making constructive choices.
	Knows how to keep self and others safe in a variety of situations.	Knows how to keep themselves safe in most situations.	Is capable of being safe, but sometimes is not.
	Is able to consider the consequences of their actions, both good and bad.	Is able to identify some consequences of their actions.	Struggles to anticipate possible consequences to their actions.

Comments

_____

_____

_____

Overall

☐

Connecting to Self Analysis

Directions: Record each student's overall symbols (page 199) in the appropriate columns. At a glance, you can view: (1) which students need more help mastering these skills and (2) how students progress throughout the school year.

Student Name	Week 6	Week 12	Week 18	Week 24	Week 30	Week 36

Relating to Others Analysis

Directions: Record each student's overall symbols (page 200) in the appropriate columns. At a glance, you can view: (1) which students need more help mastering these skills and (2) how students progress throughout the school year.

Student Name	Week 6	Week 12	Week 18	Week 24	Week 30	Week 36

Making Decisions Analysis

Directions: Record each student's overall symbols (page 201) in the appropriate columns. At a glance, you can view: (1) which students need more help mastering these skills and (2) how students progress throughout the school year.

Student Name	Week 6	Week 12	Week 18	Week 24	Week 30	Week 36